FIRST TIMOTHY

Pure Heart
Good Conscience
Sincere Faith

•

FRANK M. BARKER, JR.

Prepared for
Associate Reformed Presbyterian
Women of the Church
Bible Study for 1998

GREAT COMMISSION PUBLICATIONS

ISBN 0-934688-86-9

Printed in USA

Published by Great Commission Publications
3640 Windsor Park Drive, Suite 100
Suwanee, GA 30024-1800

CONTENTS

PREFACE

The Church is God's instrument for advancing his kingdom, spreading the gospel, conserving its fruit, and having an uplifting effect even on non-Christian society. How crucial it is that we have strong local churches in every culture and place.

Paul's first letter to Timothy deals with how we can develop strong local churches. He tells Timothy what his goals for his people should be. He speaks of the seriousness of being entrusted with the gospel and the need to preserve it undiluted—and then to propagate it. He emphasizes the danger of false teachers and how to keep strong spiritually. What could be more relevant in our day of widespread defection from the truth in the church and of accommodation to a growing immorality and relativism in society?

Paul's emphasis on the place of prayer in the church and on standards for church leadership are still needed today! He also deals with areas that are the source of great controversy currently, such as the place of women in ministry. His treatment of the use of material resources is especially needed in our materialistic society. Following the principles Paul gives here will revitalize our lives and our churches.

Let's dive in!

PUBLISHER'S NOTE

The Appendix at the end of this book is crucial. It is a chapter from the book *Living in Christ's Church* by Edmund P. Clowney, published by Great Commission Publications. We include it in this book on 1 Timothy so that you will get a comprehensive, biblical view of the general and special offices in the church.

When you grasp that concept, you will begin to see in fresh ways how 1 Timothy applies to all church members in general and not only to elders and deacons in particular. Lay people will be encouraged by understanding that in the general office of believers they can function in many of the ways in which others serve in the special offices in the church.

To understand this, and to see the significance of both the general and special offices in the church, take time to read this Appendix. This can have a profoundly biblical impact on your service to the Lord in the days ahead.

1

The Goal of the Gospel
1 Timothy 1:1–10

Since the eighteenth century, commentators and church leaders have referred to Paul's letters to Timothy and Titus as the Pastoral Epistles because they deal with directions for pastors and congregational life. Actually, Timothy and Titus functioned as special envoys for Paul; they were more like troubleshooters than settled pastors. Nevertheless, a study of Paul's first letter to Timothy is crucial today. His epistle sheds light on important matters of local church organization and operation—so that "you will know how people ought to conduct themselves in God's household" (1 Tim. 3:15).

Paul discusses such things as the place of God's law in the Christian's life, what believers should pray for and how they can pray effectively, the role of women in the church, qualifications for leaders and how to develop them, how to handle false teachers, how to counsel people regarding their material resources—and similar subjects. What could be more relevant or practical?

The Salutation (1:1–4)

The opening greeting identifies Paul as the author of this letter (vs. 1). Some scholars question his authorship since the book of Acts closes with Paul in Rome under house arrest awaiting trial. Paul himself, however, indicates in 1 Timothy 3:14 that he hopes to visit Timothy soon. Apparently what happened was that Paul stood trial, was acquitted and then later was arrested again. When he writes his second letter to Timothy, he is facing death (2 Tim. 1:8; 4:6, 7). In William Hendriksen's view Paul was released in A.D. 63. He then traveled to Ephesus and left Timothy there. From Ephesus he went to Macedonia, where he wrote this epistle to Timothy.[1]

Paul strikes a note of authority as he mentions his apostleship. The term *apostle* can have a broad sense, but here Paul uses it in a restricted sense. Paul was made an apostle "by the command of God our Savior." Usually it is Christ who is referred to as the Savior, but it is helpful to remember the saving activity of God the Father.

On occasion, individuals twist the gospel and picture God the Father only as an avenging judge who has his rod lifted, ready to strike us. In this view Christ thwarts the intentions of the Father and casts himself between, taking the blow designed for us. Sometimes these individuals use the story of Pocahontas as an illustration. This daughter of the Indian chief Powhatan fell in love with John Smith, one of the early pilgrims in America. When Powhatan became enraged and raised his club to strike John Smith, Pocahontas threw herself between her father and Smith to take the blow. This is not a good illustration of the gospel. For the example to work, Powhatan should have taken his own blow, for Christ and the Father work together in our salvation. God so loved the world that he sent his Son and thus took our punishment himself in the person of Jesus Christ.

> 'Twas not to make Jehovah's love
> Toward his people flame,
> That Jesus from his throne above
> A suffering man became.
> 'Twas not the death which he endured,
> Nor all the pangs he bore,
> That God's eternal love procured,
> For God was love before. [2]

Paul refers to Christ as our hope. *Hope* in the New Testament connotes something that is certain but future. We are certain about Christ's return, about our bodies being raised from the grave and about ultimately living in a new heaven and earth. But for those without Christ, life is hopeless (Eph. 2:12).

Paul addresses this letter to Timothy (vs. 2), whom Paul refers to as "my true son in the faith." Paul had not led him to Christ (see 2 Tim. 1:5; 3:15), but he evidently had trained him (Acts 16:1–5). Paul desires grace, mercy and peace for him. Paul had urged Timothy to stay at Ephesus to help that church (vs. 3). He was to "command certain men not to teach false doctrines any longer." This statement presupposes a recognized standard of Christian teaching. Timothy was also to put a stop to unprofitable teaching—"myths and endless genealogies" (vs. 4). This teaching, which apparently had a Jewish background, produced more doubts than faith; it promoted "controversies rather than God's work."

What is the result of *your* teaching? Do people believe the Scripture more? trust God more? desire him more? What about the teaching you are receiving—what is its nature and effect?

The term *myths* (Greek *mythoi,* a fiction, a fable, a falsehood) brings to mind the false teaching that says many of the key events recorded in Scripture—such as the creation of Adam and Eve, the fall, the flood, the virgin birth and the resurrection of Christ—are myths; these stories might convey helpful lessons, but they certainly aren't historical events. Bishop John A. T. Robinson of the Church of England in his book *But That I Can't Believe* discusses the reality of the incarnation. He says that the Gospel writers communicated the truth that God was in Christ "in the only way they knew, by giving the whole story a glow of glory, a brush of wings, a touch of sheer miracle," but that the events celebrated at Christmas are "not a literal account of how things happened." Speaking of the resurrection of Christ, Robinson says the New Testament "is silent" about what happened to his body! "But even if the corpse was somewhere around, as the cocoon is somewhere around when the butterfly has flown, it was as nothing to his friends any longer."

One of my seminary professors once challenged me, saying, "When they dig up Jesus' body in Palestine, it's going to destroy your faith." I said, "You're right that my faith is based on the resurrection of Christ. But they're not going to dig up his body!"

To get some feel of the radical difference between the Gospel accounts and myths, consider the following paragraph from the so-called Gospel of Peter that originated in the second century:

> And in the night...as the soldiers kept guard two by two, there was a great voice in heaven; and they saw the heavens opened and two men descend from thence with great light and approach the tomb. And that stone which was put at the door rolled away of its own accord....When therefore the soldiers saw it, they awakened the centurion and the elders, for they too were hard-by keeping guard. And as they declared what things they had seen, again they see three men come forth from the tomb, two of them supporting one, and a cross followed them. And of the two the head reached unto the heaven, but the head of him who was led by them overpassed the heavens. And they heard a voice from the heavens say-

ing, "Hast thou preached to them that sleep?" And a response was heard from the cross, "Yes." [3]

The Subject (1:5–10)

Paul now addresses the goal of the gospel, the swerving of some from that goal and the proper use of the law.

First, Paul speaks of the goal of the gospel: "The goal of this command is love, which comes from a pure heart" (vs. 5). The "command" could refer to the law (and love is the fulfilling of the law), but Paul's reference to a "pure heart" makes it more likely that he is talking about the gospel. The law can't produce a pure heart or the love that the law commands (see Rom. 8:3, 4). The whole object of the gospel and of the law is that we might love God and our neighbors. The goal of the gospel is not just to save us from hell but also to renew us in the image of Christ and make us loving. (1 Corinthians 13 describes this love in detail.) A pure heart, a good conscience and a sincere faith bring forth this love.

We don't naturally have pure hearts. Jesus said, "Out of the heart come evil thoughts, murder, adultery, sexual immorality" (Matt. 15:19). But when I became a Christian, my heart was purified. That's exactly what Ezekiel said would happen: "I will give you a new heart and put a new spirit in you; I will remove from you your heart of stone and give you a heart of flesh. And I will put my Spirit in you and move you to follow my decrees and be careful to keep my laws" (Ezek. 36:26, 27).

A good conscience is one that has received forgiveness

through Christ. The light of Scripture corrects and informs the conscience so that it will follow the dictates of the Bible. As we maintain a good conscience we will demonstrate love in our lives.

A sincere faith—the root of the whole—is when persons put their genuine, unpretended confidence in Jesus Christ. This means that not only do they *believe* the claims of Christ to be God, to have become man, to have died in their stead and to have risen from the dead, but they also *trust* Christ to forgive them and to save them.

A pure heart, a good conscience and a sincere faith provide the ground out of which the Holy Spirit—now living in me in union with my human spirit—brings forth the fruit of love. I now have the ability to love God and my neighbor. Not perfectly, of course, because I still have a surviving—though not reigning—sinful nature. But still, practically and progressively, I love!

Second, Paul mentions that some people have strayed from this goal of love: "Some have wandered away from these and turned to meaningless talk" (vs. 6). You cannot produce love apart from the ground from which it comes: a pure heart, a good conscience, loyalty to the truth and a determination to submit your reason to God's revelation. Some people wanted prominence as teachers of the law (vs. 7), but they really didn't know what they were talking about or affirming. Their wandering showed up in their teaching legalism, adding to the commandments of God the doctrines of men (see 4:3–8).

Finally, Paul discusses the use of the law (vss. 8–10). He

says the law was not made for a righteous person but "for lawbreakers and rebels, the ungodly and sinful," and then he gives a long list of such people, basically following the outline of the Ten Commandments. As Hendriksen says, "If I am so good that I just naturally keep the law, then I do not need the law." But who of us is like that? Paul says this catalog of sins applies to him (vs. 15). Who has not lusted after another person in his heart (which is adultery or fornication)? Or who has not broken the commandment to honor his parents? Our comfort is that Christ died for the ungodly (Rom. 5:8).

The law was made for all of us! Its purpose is threefold:

(1) to restrain our wickedness. When the law says, "The soul who sins is the one who will die" (Ezek. 18:4), it keeps me from doing some things I might otherwise do.

(2) to reveal our guilt—"through the law we become conscious of sin" (Rom. 3:20). Isaac Watts put it this way:

> My guilt appeared but small before,
> 'Til terribly I saw
> How perfect, holy, just and pure
> Was thine eternal law!

(3) to be a rule for us to live by once we have been renewed by Christ. Calvin, commenting on the law in the believer's life, says:

> For even though they have the law written and engraved upon their hearts by the finger of God,

16

that is, have been so moved and quickened through the directing of the Spirit that they long to obey God, they still profit from the law in two ways.

Here is the best instrument for them *to learn more thoroughly each day the nature of the Lord's will* to which they aspire, and to confirm them in the understanding of it....

Again, because we need not only teaching but also exhortation, the servant of God will also avail himself of this benefit of the law: by frequent meditation upon it *to be aroused to obedience...*, and be drawn back from the slippery path of transgression.[4]

The Summary

The ultimate goal of the gospel is to make us loving, obedient followers of Christ. This means that by the power of God's Spirit we use the law of God as our daily guide, seeking to live by the Ten Commandments and the law of love (1 Corinthians 13) and repenting when we fail. Since that is what Christ died for, is that your goal? In what area do you fall short of showing love?

Remember also what undermines our growth—false and unprofitable teaching that deals with irrelevancies and promotes doubts. Do you expose yourself to this kind of teaching? The only ground that produces genuine love is a pure heart, a good conscience and a sincere faith. Has your heart been made pure? Is your conscience tuned to the law of

God? Have you placed your trust in Christ?

Review Questions

1. What were the reasons that Paul wrote this letter to Timothy? What were the historical circumstances under which it was written?

2. Why is the illustration of Pocahontas not a good one to illustrate Christ's atonement?

3. What does it mean to have faith in Jesus Christ?

4. What is the goal of the gospel?

5. Where can we find a description of what love looks like? What is the source of such love?

6. What is the proper use of the Ten Commandments?

2

Entrusted with the Good News
1 Timothy 1:11–20

What is the most precious thing ever committed to your trust? What personal quality or characteristic is most needed for carrying out that responsibility? Paul answers those questions concerning himself while writing to Timothy, whom he had asked to do some pastoral troubleshooting for the Ephesian congregation.

Christ Entrusted Paul with the Good News (1:11–17)

The object entrusted to Paul was "the glorious gospel of the blessed God" (vs. 11). The word *gospel* means good news, and that's what it is—a body of information about what God has done to restore ruined, rebellious sinners to his favor. Listen to Paul summarize this good news— "I want to remind you of the gospel…: that Christ died for our sins according to the Scriptures, that he was bur-

19

ied, that he was raised on the third day according to the Scriptures..." (1 Cor. 15:1, 3, 4). Christ died for our sins—there is the heart of the gospel. Isaac Watts responded by writing in "Alas! and Did My Savior Bleed":

> Well might the sun in darkness hide,
> And shut his glories in,
> When Christ, the mighty Maker, died
> For man the creature's sin.

This precious news is also entrusted to us. When people hear and respond to this news, God restores them to his favor. The gospel is God's cure for the spiritual disease that has infected the human race. What is expected of those who have been entrusted with this cure? Paul responds, "I thank Christ Jesus our Lord, who has given me strength, that he considered me faithful, appointing me to his service" (vs. 12). Bearers of the gospel are not required to be brilliant or original or even successful, but they are expected to be faithful. Christ expects them to preserve the gospel and to pass it on intact, not altering it in any way. If they change the formula, it will lose its ability to cure.

The wonder drugs that cure diseases often have unpleasant side effects—nausea, for example. Picture a conversation between two doctors, one of whom desires to remove the ingredient of a drug that causes nausea. The other doctor says, "No, we cannot remove that because then the drug would no longer cure."

So it is with the gospel. True, it has its unpalatable aspects. It tells us we are guilty sinners and that apart from

Jesus Christ we are doomed to a horrible eternity. The proud find that hard to swallow. The gospel tells us that we have to repent, turn from our sins, and surrender our will to Jesus Christ as our Lord and trust him as our Savior. People want to remove some of these offensive elements, but if they do, the gospel loses its curative power.

It is not enough, however, to preserve the gospel intact. Faithfulness also requires that we propagate it. If we had a cure for a fatal disease and we did not share it, we would be guilty of terrible selfishness. The majority of the human race have never been offered God's remedy for their fatal spiritual disease! Paul says that Jesus Christ counted him faithful to carry out his assignment. As an apostle, Paul had a special ministry. Likewise every Christian has a ministry. Paul teaches that God gives gifted leaders to the church "to prepare God's people for works of service" (Eph. 4:12).

Each believer is obligated to preserve and propagate this wonderful gospel formula. Not only did Christ expect Paul to be faithful, but he enabled him to be fruitful—"I thank Christ Jesus...who has given me strength" (vs. 12). Christ gives the command, and Christ enables us to fulfill the command. This is the most incredible aspect of the good news: Jesus Christ comes and lives in us to remake us and to enable us to carry out his mission!

But we must pray for the strength to serve Christ. When Charles Spurgeon was a teenager, the New Park Street Baptist Church in London called him to be their pastor. He told his congregation that they and other churches lacked power because God had withheld his face from them. He said that apart from the enablement of God, the kingdom could not be extended in their midst. He challenged them to "cry to the Lord until he reveals his face again." They did, and before long there was a great stirring in that congregation. When asked the secret of his power, Spurgeon replied, "My people pray for me."[1]

Does it strike you as odd that Christ entrusted Paul with the gospel? Look at the reference to Paul's old life (vs. 13). He was a blasphemer who ridiculed the name of Jesus, and he persecuted Christians—even having them killed. But then he says that he was shown mercy. The one entrusted with the precious formula of the gospel had experienced its curative power.

Paul now gives the reasons he was shown mercy. One factor was Paul's ignorance (vs. 13); he didn't realize his own guilty state and character. He thought he was faultless before the law (Phil. 3:6). He wasn't aware of who Jesus really was, believing him to be an imposter whose disciples had lied about his resurrection. When Paul says that he obtained mercy because he acted in ignorance, he implies that had he done those things knowingly, he would have so hardened his heart that he would have committed the unpardonable sin (see Matt. 12:31, 32).

A second factor was Christ's grace "poured out on me abundantly" (vs. 14). Grace refers to undeserved favor. This grace came with "faith and love." When Christ called Paul by appearing to him on the road to Damascus, he created faith in Paul's heart, a faith that bore the fruit of love—love for Christ and others. Grace does the same for us today.

A third reason Christ showed mercy to Paul was that Christ's purpose in coming into the world was to save sinners (vs. 15). Paul says that this is "a trustworthy saying that deserves full acceptance." Christ wants to demonstrate to the world his patience with sinners (vs. 16). Who then can despair? Paul is an example of the change Christ performs in the lives of all those who place their trust in him.

One of the first converts during the Reformation in England was Thomas Bilney, a student at Cambridge. Searching for God and relief for his conscience, he went to a priest who advised fasting, long vigils, masses and indulgences. Bilney found no consolation in any of them. Secretly he purchased a Greek New Testament, a book forbidden by the church. He ran to his room, and when he opened the volume, his eyes fell on this verse 15. He meditated on the astonishing declaration. Saint Paul was the chief of sinners and yet was sure of being saved? Suddenly the light dawned. "It is Jesus Christ who saves and not the church. My vigils, my fasts, my pilgrimages...were destroying instead of saving me!"[2]

After referring to his old life and to the mercy he received, Paul reflects on God's greatness. He bursts forth in a doxology of adoration and gratitude: "Now to the King eternal, immortal, invisible, the only God, be honor and glory for ever and ever" (vs. 17). As the hymn writer Elizabeth C. Clephane expressed when she wrote "Beneath the Cross of Jesus,"

And from my stricken heart with tears
Two wonders I confess,
The wonders of redeeming love
And my unworthiness.

Paul Encouraged Timothy to Endure (1:18–20)

Paul encourages Timothy to endure in the task assigned to him (vs. 18) and refers to the ministry as a fight. This describes the service of every Christian, for Christ told his disciples that people would hate them because people hated him (Luke 21:17). Spurgeon is praised today, but he experienced conflict when he ministered in London: "Scarce a day rolls over my head in which the most villainous abuse, the most fearful slander is not uttered against me both privately and by the public press."[3]

First, Paul encourages Timothy to fight the good fight by remembering the prophecies about him (vs. 18). When elders set Timothy apart for the ministry, God gave prophecies through some that were present (see 4:14). These prophecies probably indicated that God had called Timothy, told him that he would suffer, and promised that he would see Timothy through difficult times.

Next, Paul tells Timothy to fight the good fight by relying on God to protect and empower him (vs. 19). The Amplified New Testament translates "holding on to faith" as "keeping fast hold on faith (that leaning of the entire human personality on God in absolute trust and confidence)." In other words, just keep on trusting in God regardless of the forces that are lined up against you. Of

24

course by continuing to trust God, Timothy would also refuse to change the message of the gospel or compromise his conscience. "Holding on to faith" could include the idea of "keep clinging to the truth of the gospel"—God's Word (Hendriksen). Don't adjust Scripture to suit the fancies of people; call on them to conform to it.

Paul warns against compromise by naming two men who shipwrecked their faith when they cast aside their rudder of conscience (vs. 20a). The same Thomas Bilney referred to earlier became one of the early lights of the Reformation in England. Authorities summoned him and commanded him to recant or be burned at the stake. His friends also urged him to recant and save his life in order to dedicate it to spreading the truth later. Bilney became confused, and his faith wavered. Under the pretext of being useful to Christ for many more years, Bilney publicly rejected what he had learned from the Bible. Then, having denied the Word of God, he could no longer endure hearing it.

How much better to be like Martin Luther who, when faced with a similar situation, replied,

> My conscience is bound by the Word of God. It
> is a dangerous thing to go against the conscience.
> Here I stand; I can do no other. God help me.
> Amen!

And God preserved Luther and used him to turn the world upside down!

Paul mentions that the disciplinary action inflicted on Hymenaeus and Alexander included being "handed over to Satan to be taught not to blaspheme" (vs. 20b). Apparently this refers to excommunication—being put out of the church into Satan's province, the world (see 1 Cor. 5:5, 13). At any rate, the purpose—"to be taught not to blaspheme"—was to restore them so that they might receive mercy.

It's encouraging to note that after a period of time, Thomas Bilney was restored to fellowship with God and began preaching the truth once more. Again the authorities gave him the choice of recanting or being burned. This time he chose the stake and even kissed it, proclaiming: "It is a privilege to die for the truth."

You and I stand in a position similar to that of Paul and Timothy. Let's be just as earnest about preserving and publicizing God's cure for sinners by all means possible. Note carefully the connection between maintaining the faith and a good conscience. Don't water down the message in any way. Don't compromise your conscience in any area. Be sure that you have experienced the grace that was poured out on the chief of sinners.

Review Questions

1. What is the gospel?

2. What are some of the unpalatable aspects of the gospel?

3. What does God require those entrusted with the gospel to do?

4. What are some reasons why Paul received mercy?

5. How did Paul encourage Timothy to endure hard times?

3

Shhh! They're Praying

1 Timothy 2:1–8

Why do many evangelical churches lack power? Is there any common denominator in churches where God is moving powerfully? While dynamic churches may vary considerably in certain doctrines and practices, they are praying churches. And any study of the history of revivals demonstrates that they occur when Christians pray.

In a recent capital funds campaign in our church, we placed a green wooden chair on the platform Sunday after Sunday. This was because of something that occurred in the early days of our church. It started when a gentleman who was attending our church came to me with a problem. "Friend," I said, "the only solution to that problem is prayer."

"I don't much believe there is a God," he responded. "In any case he certainly doesn't answer prayer!"

A group of men from the church met regularly on

Wednesday nights for prayer, and we had seen God answer prayer. I explained this to the man and invited him to join us. Surprisingly, he agreed. When we met the next Wednesday, he said to the group, "I don't want to be here under false pretenses. I don't believe God answers prayers, but I'd like to believe it. Frank has told me you pray for specific things and have seen answers. I'd like to watch."

"Did you have something specific in mind?" the group asked him.

"Yes," he replied. "Frank said you prayed for better attendance at church and saw it increase. But attendance is down now."

"It's the middle of summer," they answered. "Everyone's on vacation."

"What about all those people who aren't going to church?" he said. "Just ask God to bring them."

The group began to discuss it. Then the man added, "I want you to ask God to fill the church this Sunday."

At the time, we were running about two-thirds full, and there was no prospect of the church (which was meeting in a shopping center) filling up before fall. The group decided, however, to act on the man's request. But before they did, they said, "We need to agree on what we mean by the church being full."

The skeptic had the answer: "You'll have to bring out the green chairs." He was talking about some old wooden chairs that someone had given to us. We had painted the chairs green and were using them in Sunday school. In the past we'd needed to bring those green chairs into the worship room only on Easter.

"You're making this tough!" the group told the man.

"Do you believe?" he asked them.

"We believe," they answered.

The man then made them promise not to urge anyone to attend church beyond what they normally would do and not to tell anyone about this prayer request until after the worship service. Well—we prayed. Sunday came, and the church wasn't even two-thirds filled. But as I stood up to lead the opening prayer, I looked through the plate glass window of the storefront, and I saw a lot of cars starting to turn into the parking lot. By the time I had finished praying, a crowd was at the door. The next thing you know the ushers were bringing in the green chairs! God had moved in answer to believing prayer. Many times since then, God has answered as our congregation has asked.

The Exhortation to Pray (2:1, 2a)

Paul stresses to Timothy the importance of getting people to pray (vs. l). Actually, when we look at the end of this section, we see that Paul is dealing with what men should do in public worship: "I want men everywhere to lift up holy hands in prayer..." (vs. 8). How important it is that *men* pray! Men are sometimes prone to delegate praying to their wives or other women. But God has placed men as the leaders of their families and the church, and they should lead in this crucial matter of prayer.

Prayer is hard work. We saw exciting things happen in that prayer group that I mentioned above, but I noticed that on cold winter mornings when we would gather at 7 A.M. on Saturdays at the church (we changed from the evening to the morning when we acquired our first building), there would be only three of us present: myself, my associate pastor and the chairman of the board of deacons. One Saturday a month, however, the women in the church took turns cooking breakfast for the men, and we would have 40 or 50 present!

"I think it has something to do with eating!" I told my wife. "But I don't feel like asking the women to get up every Saturday at 5:30 A.M. to cook breakfast." And bless her heart, my wife took my not-so-subtle hint and said that she didn't mind helping to prepare breakfast for the men. So I said to the fellows, "Let's meet the other three Saturdays at our home. We'll pray first and then have breakfast."

The first Saturday, 17 men came. When attendance grew to 36, one man said, "It's getting crowded around here! Why don't some of you meet at my home?" And another said, "I'd enjoy having a group at my house." And now we have five such groups that meet on Saturday mornings. I really believe that some of the most significant work of our church is taking place right in these groups!

Paul mentions four types of prayer: requests, prayers, intercession and thanksgiving (vs. 1). *Requests* refer to prayers for specific things—perhaps the congregation has a financial need, or a church member needs a job. The term *prayers* is more general and points to ongoing needs, such as love and patience. *Intercession* refers to earnest petition on behalf of others; perhaps there is a serious illness or a difficult family problem. And we are to offer *thanksgiving* for God's blessings and for answered prayers.

In particular, Paul urges prayer for the government—"for kings and all those in authority" (vs. 2a). The evil Nero was emperor of Rome at this time. He later burned some Christians at the stake and fed others to the lions. Paul certainly called for a full-orbed approach to prayer on the part of the local church!

What place does prayer have in *your* life? What is your church doing in this area, and are you involved? Men, how do you lead your family in prayer?

Prayer and the World (2:2b–7)

Paul gives reasons why Christians should pray for the government. First, good government promotes peace. Paul wants us to "live peaceful and quiet lives in all godliness and holiness" (vs. 2b). An ordered society that promotes justice in the administration of law and is free from internal disturbances is vital for the development of human society. Conditions in many of our inner cities cry out for government officials to act biblically.

Second, Christians should pray for the government to rule righteously because this promotes the will of God (vs. 3). Christianity can exist and spread under persecution, as it does in China, but it is also true that persecution may hinder the spread of the gospel. For instance, consider the difficulty that missionaries have in taking the gospel to Muslim nations. Normally the church flourishes better in an ordered and peaceful society where persons are free to consider the claims of Christ without the threat of persecution.

Paul then gets right to the heart of why Christians should pray for good government: God "wants all men to be saved and to come to a knowledge of the truth" (vs. 4). God's desire is that all people be saved. Some people, conscious of the biblical teaching of election, feel that believers should interpret a statement like this as meaning not that God desires the salvation of all people but that he desires the salvation of all types of people from all ranks and from all nations. We need not shrink back, however, from affirming that God desires the salvation of all persons. After a painstaking study of all related Scriptures, Ned Stonehouse and John Murray concluded:

> We have found that God himself expresses an ardent desire for the fulfillment of certain things which he has not decreed in his inscrutable counsel to come to pass....This is indeed mysterious, and why he has not brought to pass, in the exercise of his omnipotent power and grace, what is his ardent pleasure lies hid in the sovereign counsel of his will. We should not entertain, however, any prejudice against the notion that God desires or has pleasure in the accomplishment of what he does not decretively will....We found that God reveals himself as not taking pleasure in or desiring the death of those who die but rather as taking pleasure in or desiring the repentance and

life of the wicked. This will of God to repentance and salvation is universalized and reveals to us, therefore, that there is in God a benevolent lovingkindness towards the repentance and salvation of even those whom he has not decreed to save. This pleasure, will, desire is expressed in the universal call to repentance.[1]

A dramatic illustration of this desire is seen in Jesus weeping over Jerusalem and saying, "O Jerusalem, Jerusalem... how often I have longed to gather your children together, as a hen gathers her chicks...but you were not willing" (Matt. 23:37; compare Luke 19:41, 42). What a powerful demonstration of the fact that God desires that all people be saved!

Salvation is a many-faceted biblical concept. If I am being swept down a river, I simply need to be saved from going over the waterfall. But when I am a guilty sinner, I need salvation from the punishment that is due me for breaking God's holy law. And I need the bondage of sin in my life broken. I am also alienated from God and spiritually dead. Salvation then involves the removal of my guilt and being counted righteous in the sight of God. It also means being set free from the domination of sin in my life. It includes reconciliation with God so that I am in fellowship with him. It means being made spiritually alive. Paul says that God made us alive with Christ even when we were dead in transgressions (Eph. 2:5). God desires that people experience this great salvation. Oh, the wonder of it!

Jesus was accused of associating with sinners. In response he told a series of three parables: one about a shepherd who had lost a sheep but went out and found it; another about a woman who had lost a valuable coin but searched the house until she located it; and a third about a father who had lost his son to riotous living but waited to welcome him back (Luke 15). Jesus was telling us that he cares about sinners because God cares about them. He is like the shepherd, the woman and the father—he longs for the recovery of the lost one.

In order to be saved one must come "to a knowledge of the truth" (vs. 4b). There is truth that is available, and through which we come into a relationship with God. One day I sat next to a young woman at a luncheon. In the course of the conversation she said, "Don't you think we are all searching for truth?"

"I'm not," I said. "I've found it. I'm just trying to tell others what I have found." Is that presumptuous? No, it's biblical Christianity.

What is the essence of that truth? Paul tells us: "For there is one God and one mediator between God and men, the man Christ Jesus" (vs. 5). There is only one true God, but he exists in three persons. One of those persons, God the Son, became human in order to be the mediator—the go-between—through whom sinful people might approach the holy God. Paul describes the work of Christ Jesus as giving a ransom for all (vs. 6a). A ransom is something that is paid to set a prisoner free. Christ paid the price to set us free.

I sinned. And straightway, posthaste, Satan flew
    Before the presence of the most high God,
And made a railing accusation there.
    He said, "This soul, this thing of clay and sod
Has sinned. 'Tis true that he has named Thy name,
    But I demand his death, for Thou hast said,
'The soul that sinneth, it shall die.' Shall not
    Thy sentence be fulfilled? Is justice dead?
Send now this wretched sinner to his doom.
    What other thing can righteous ruler do?"
And thus he did accuse me day and night,
    And every word he spoke, Oh God, was true.

Then quickly One rose up from God's right hand,
    Before Whose glory angels veiled their eyes.
He spoke, "Each jot and tittle of the law
    Must be fulfilled; the guilty sinner dies!
But wait—suppose his guilt were all transferred
    To Me, and that I paid his penalty!
Behold My hands, My side, My feet! One day
    I was made sin for him, and died that he
Might be presented faultless at Thy throne."
    And Satan flew away. Full well he knew
That he could not prevail against that love,
    For every word my dear Lord spoke was true.[2]

The scriptural teaching of the substitutionary atonement
of Christ is often challenged. David Edwards, a leading
churchman in England, says in dialogue with John Stott:

So I ask whether it is "the" necessary meaning of the atonement that "in and through Christ crucified God substituted himself for us and bore our sins" and "took his own loving initiative to appease his own righteous anger by bearing it his own self in his own Son when he took our place and died for us" (CoC, p. 175). What do the Scriptures say? I cannot find Dr. Stott's theory taught plainly anywhere in them. If it is "the heart of the gospel," is it not extremely strange that it is not mentioned in any of the gospels?[3]

Stott's answer is that the substitutionary atonement of Christ is plainly taught—directly or indirectly—everywhere in the Bible. Jesus says, "I am the good shepherd. The good shepherd lays down his life for the sheep" (John 10:11). Peter explains that Jesus "bore our sins in his body on the tree…; by his wounds you have been healed" (1 Pet. 2:24). Paul says there is one mediator between God and man.

I can be tolerant of other approaches to God and intolerant of Christ, or I can be tolerant of Christ and intolerant of other approaches. I choose the latter. The only way a person can be saved is by coming to a "knowledge of the truth" of Jesus being the one mediator through his death for our sins. Actually, a better translation is "to come to the acknowledgment of the truth" (Hendriksen). To come to God through the one mediator, Jesus Christ, I must believe the claims of Christ and place my trust in him as my Savior. I also must surrender my will to him as my Master.

Paul says Jesus "gave himself as a ransom for all men—the testimony given in its proper time" (vs. 6). This amazing truth is to be told to the world. So Paul goes on to say that God appointed him a herald (a preacher) and an apostle to proclaim this (vs. 7). His particular sphere of responsibility was to be a teacher to the Gentiles. Since all the world is guilty and there is only one way of salvation, how crucial it is that we take this life-giving message to all! As the hymn "O Zion, Haste" states it,

> Behold how many thousands still are lying,
> Bound in the darksome prison-house of sin,
> With none to tell them of the Savior's dying,
> Or of the life he died for them to win.

Are we telling others of that mediator and his ransom payment?

The Conditions of Effective Prayer (2:8)

Paul returns to his exhortation about prayer, now describing the necessary conditions for prayers to be effective. When men pray, they are "to lift up holy hands in prayer, without anger or disputing." Men of old commonly lifted their hands toward heaven with their palms open as if to receive while they prayed. Scripture mentions many different bodily positions in prayer—from bowing, to standing, to kneeling, to lying face down. All are appropriate. The crucial thing is that our hands be holy. Having spiritually impure hands due to unconfessed sin in our lives is a barrier between us and God (see Ps. 66:18). When anger and arguments hurt our relationships with others, they also hurt our praying. Christ tells us, "When you stand praying, if you hold anything against anyone, forgive him, so that your Father in heaven may forgive you your sins" (Mark 11:25). Wrong attitudes in our hearts toward others make our prayers unacceptable to God.

There are other conditions of effective prayer mentioned elsewhere: we should pray in faith (Mark 11:24), with perseverance (Luke 11:8), for things according to God's will (1 John 5:14) and with Christ's word abiding in us (John 15:7).

What place does prayer have in your life? Does your church gather for prayer? Do you think that God might want you to initiate something? Are you praying for governmental authorities? Are your prayers being hindered by sin in your life? Since you realize there is only one mediator, are you involved in getting the word out? Have you, in fact, personally acknowledged that one Mediator?

Review Questions

1. Why is it important to pray for government authorities?

2. How do you reconcile the statement that God desires all persons to be saved with the doctrine of election?

3. Why was it necessary that Jesus give himself as a ransom?

4. How do people actually appropriate salvation through Christ's work as mediator?

5. What are the conditions of effective prayer?

4

What's a Woman to Do?
1 Timothy 2:9–15

The role of women in the church is a controversial issue today. Churches are ordaining women as ministers more frequently, while the Southern Baptist Church expelled a congregation in Memphis for calling a woman pastor. Some within evangelical Christianity increasingly oppose the biblical concept of male leadership in the church and in the home. Several outstanding books that shed light on scriptural considerations are *The New Testament Teaching on the Role Relationship of Men and Women* by George W. Knight III, *Man and Woman in Biblical Perspective* by James B. Hurley and *Recovering Biblical Manhood and Womanhood,* edited by John Piper and Wayne Grudem.[1]

Paul's first letter to Timothy describes how people ought to conduct themselves in church (3:15). He starts this topic by giving instructions on the role of women in the church.

How's a Woman to Dress? (2:9, 10)

Paul says women should "dress modestly, with decency and propriety" (vs. 9). Modesty indicates an unwillingness to go beyond proper bounds. Christians don't have to balk at the latest fashion—there is no virtue in being out of style—unless what is fashionable is indecent. Deciding whether a change in fashion is actually immoral is not always an easy question. C. S. Lewis in *Mere Christianity* has some helpful thoughts on this issue:

> The Christian rule of chastity must not be confused with the social rule of "modesty" (in one sense of that word); i.e. propriety, or decency. The social rule of propriety lays down how much of the human body should be displayed...according to the customs of a given social circle. Thus, while the rule of chastity is the same for all Christians at all times, the rule of propriety changes. A girl in the Pacific islands wearing hardly any clothes and a Victorian lady completely covered in clothes might both be equally "modest," proper or decent, according to the standards of their own societies: and both, for all we could tell by their dress, might be equally chaste (or equally unchaste)....When people break the rule of propriety current in their own time and place, if they do so in order to excite lust in themselves or others, then they are offending against chastity.[2]

The matter of cost is also a part of modesty. Paul says

women should not dress "with braided hair or gold or pearls or expensive clothes." He is not saying that women shouldn't have their hair fixed nicely, or try to look attractive, or wear any jewelry. In his day expensive hairdos were fashionable. Women studded their hair with gold and pearls. While dressing appropriately today, Christians also need to be good stewards of their material resources—not spending money on objects that will soon pass away, when the money could be working to evangelize a lost world or to help the poor. Christian women should be clothed "with good deeds, appropriate for women who profess to worship God" (vs. 10). This is similar to the apostle's teaching in 1 Peter 3:3, 4—

> Your beauty should not come from outward adornment, such as braided hair and the wearing of gold jewelry and fine clothes. Instead, it should be that of your inner self, the unfading beauty of a gentle and quiet spirit, which is of great worth in God's sight.

How's a Woman to Act? (2:11–15)

Paul says, "A woman should learn in quietness and full submission" (vs. 11). The quietness here means a quiet receptivity. It is not a total silence. In 1 Corinthians 11:5 Paul permits women to pray and prophesy in public worship. But he does not allow a woman to be in an authoritative teaching position over a man. "I do not permit a woman to teach or to have authority over a man; she must be silent" (vs. 12). Piper and Grudem describe the teaching that is inappropriate for a woman as teaching men "in settings or ways that dishonor the calling of men to bear the primary responsibility for teaching and leadership."[3]

The issue is not therefore whether women are competent to teach and lead, but how they do so in their relationship to men in the church. How then do we apply this principle today? It obviously rules out women holding the office of minister or ruling elder. It would seem also to indicate that women should not normally teach mixed adult Sunday school classes. An exception might be when the subject lends itself to a woman's viewpoint, such as a husband and wife team teaching on the family. We should try to adhere to the principle without becoming nitpickers.

It has been my experience that many women appreciate it when men assume and carry out their proper biblical role in the home and church. Unfortunately, if women take the lead, some men may let them and will not themselves develop into the godly leaders of the home and church that God called them to be.

But isn't this principle just a cultural adaptation due to the position of women in Paul's day and not intended to be a permanent norm? No, because when Paul gives his reasons for the principle, he grounds it not in culture but in creation. First, Paul reminds his readers of the order of creation: "For Adam was formed first, then Eve" (vs. 13). Paul sees this as indicating the headship that man is to have over woman. This, and the fact that God created woman to be man's helper, points to the submission God intended her to show in the relationship (compare 1 Cor. 11:3–10).

The headship of man is a creation mandate. It did not begin with the fall and therefore was not done away with in Christ.

The second reason Paul gives is the order of Satan's deception: "And Adam was not the one deceived; it was the woman who was deceived and became a sinner" (vs. 14). Eve's transgression occurred when she ignored her divinely ordained position. Instead of following, she chose to lead. James Hurley paraphrases Paul's point:

> The man, upon whom lay responsibility for leadership in the home and in religious matters, was prepared by God to discern the serpent's lies. The woman was not appointed religious leader and was not prepared to discern them. She was taken in. Christian worship involves re-establishing the creational pattern with men faithfully teaching God's truth and women receptively listening.[4]

Paul's commands in this area of human life are not temporary but permanent. The authority of Scripture is at stake, for as Paul claimed in a similar context, "If anybody thinks he is a prophet or spiritually gifted, let him acknowledge that what I am writing to you is the Lord's command" (1 Cor. 14:37).

The apostle closes this section with a difficult statement about the possibility of women's salvation: "But women will be saved through childbearing—if they continue in faith, love and holiness with propriety" (vs. 15). It's possible that childbirth is a reference to the birth of Jesus, the Seed who crushed the serpent's head. Douglas Moo interprets the verse in a different way:

> We think it is preferable to view verse 15 as designating the circumstances in which Christian women will experience (work out; see Philippians 2:12) their salvation—in maintaining as priorities those key roles that Paul, in keeping with Scripture elsewhere, highlights: being faithful, helpful wives, raising children to love and reverence God, managing the household.[5]

How Does This Square with…?

Questions will probably still come to mind. For instance, Paul says that "there is neither Jew nor Greek, slave nor free, male nor female, for you are all one in Christ Jesus" (Gal. 3:28). In that context, Paul is saying that all believers are equally made "sons of God through faith in Christ Jesus" (3:26). We must not set Paul in opposition to Paul or we negate the inspiration of Scripture. Certainly women united to Christ are fully equal to men in status before God—and in importance. Paul simply isn't dealing in Galatians with the relationship between men and women in terms of headship.

A second question might be, "What about when God raised up Deborah to lead Israel?" In commenting on 1 Timothy 2:9–15 John Calvin says, "If any one bring forward, by way of objection, Deborah…the answer is easy. Extraordinary acts done by God do not overturn the ordinary rules of government, by which he intended that we should be bound."

But didn't Priscilla teach Apollos? Yes, in Acts 18:26 we read that Priscilla and Aquila took the gifted preacher Apollos aside "and explained to him the way of God more adequately." This was private teaching, not the public teaching that Paul forbids in 1 Timothy 2:12. I had such an experience: I once requested Elizabeth Newbold, a very gifted teacher, to instruct me privately about the scriptural teaching of being filled with the Holy Spirit. To my dying day I will be indebted to her for her teaching!

Does sending women as missionaries violate this principle? Without question, women have played an outstanding role as missionaries. Ordinarily their ministry is basic evangelism that all Christians are to do. Paul says, "Help these women who have contended at my side in the cause of the gospel" (Phil. 4:3). There is also a difference between an emerging church and an established one. When women missionaries evangelize and a church is organized, there should be male leadership as soon as possible. We should not be sending women to be pastors or elders.

What Ministries Can Women Have?

There are unlimited opportunities for women to minister within scriptural bounds. They are to teach other women (Titus 2:3–5) and children. They are to evangelize, to disciple, to minister to the sick and needy, to organize people to fight evils in our society (such as pornography and abortion) and to write Bible study materials.

One woman in our church heads up a weekly community Bible study attended by over 400 women. Another woman engaged in a prison ministry has led a female inmate to Christ. That convert is now a key staff person for Prison Fellowship. Many women also lead neighborhood Bible clubs for children; others visit hospitals and nursing homes. A crucial ministry today for women involves counseling pregnant teenagers, sharing the gospel with them and urging them to consider adoption rather than abortion. Our church has lay counseling training that incorporates both men and women. Sports, music and drama ministries are also good areas for service. And certainly the ministry of prayer is an especially important area of service. As one can see, the opportunities are abundant!

John Piper urges women not to assume that out-of-the-home full-time employment is a better use of their time than the opportunities for service as a witness in the home, the neighborhood, the community and the church. He asks, "Which would be greater for the Kingdom—to work for someone who tells you what to do to make his or her business prosper, or to be God's free agent dreaming your own dream about how your time and your home and your creativity could make God's business prosper?"[6]

In summary, "Don't let the world around you squeeze you into its own mold, but let God remold your minds from within" (Rom. 12:2, Phillips). How knowledgeable are you about the Scriptures? Are you redeeming the time for the kingdom? If you are a woman, are you chafing under the biblical injunction for men to lead in the church, or are you encouraging men to lead while you seize your own abundant opportunities for ministry? If you are a man, are you assuming your leadership responsibilities at home and in the church?

Review Questions

1. What determines whether a style of dress is modest or decent?

2. What activities and positions in the church are women excluded from by Paul's command that forbids "a woman to teach or to have authority over a man"?

3. What ministries are open to women?

4. How would you answer someone who says that these injunctions of Paul were just cultural and temporary?

5. In the light of this passage, how would you justify sending out women missionaries?

Who's Qualified to Lead?
1 Timothy 3:1–16

Excluding ministers, who is the finest church officer you have known? What made him so effective? Was it his godly demeanor? leadership ability? caring for the flock? administrative talents? teaching ability? evangelistic zeal? What difference did his presence make in the congregation?

The Church's Officers (3:1–13)

The New Testament records different types of church officers. In 1 Timothy 3, Paul refers to overseers (vs. 1) and deacons (vs. 12). Today a bishop (an "overseer") usually has jurisdiction over a number of churches, while an elder is one of a group of men having oversight of a single church. The New Testament, however, uses both terms—elder and overseer—to refer to the same office. For instance, Paul wrote to Titus that he had left Titus in Crete to "appoint elders in every town....An elder must be blameless....Since an overseer is entrusted with God's work, he must be blameless" (Titus 1:5–7). "Elder" indicates the governing or ruling aspect of the office. (The Presbyterian church gets its name from the Greek word for elder, *presbyteros,* which indicates that elders govern the church.) "Overseer" points to the responsibility of shepherding or overseeing the flock. On one occasion Paul called for the elders of the Ephesian congregation and said, "Keep watch over yourselves and all the flock of which the Holy Spirit has made you overseers [Greek *episkopoi,* bishops]" (Acts 20:17, 28). (The Episcopal church also gets its name from its form of government, for it is ruled by bishops.)

Later in this letter to Timothy, Paul mentions elders "who direct the affairs of the church well" and also those "whose work is preaching and teaching" (5:17). So Presbyterian churches make a distinction between *ruling elders* and *teaching elders,* the latter being ordained ministers but having the same ruling authority as the former. Together they have oversight over the flock.

From Acts 6 we learn that the office of deacon came into being when the apostles' duties of ministering the Word and praying did not allow them to take on the additional responsibility of caring for widows in the Jerusalem church. These leaders told the congregation to "choose seven men...known to be full of the Holy Spirit and wisdom. We will turn this responsibility over to them" (Acts 6:3). This office was one of serving (Greek *diakonos,* a deacon, a servant), not ruling.

This account brings out the relation between the congregation and its officers. The congregation chose its officers, but the apostles then appointed them. In choosing, the congregation sought out spiritual men to whom God had given the gift of leadership. Paul explains that Christ gives gifted men to his church, and while the church prays and chooses, the Holy Spirit makes them overseers (Acts 20:28).

One time, after a local church placed a friend of mine in a leadership role, he told his wife, "I believe God put me in this position." Later, when something wasn't going as he liked, he told her that he was going to resign.

"To whom?" she asked.

"The elders," he replied.

"I thought you said God put you there," she countered.

He didn't resign!

Once the elders are in office, the congregation should follow their leadership as long as it is biblical. "Now we ask you, brothers, to respect those who work hard among you, who are over you in the Lord and who admonish you. Hold them in the highest regard in love because of their work" (1 Thess. 5:12, 13).

The Scriptures do teach a form of church government. The small details are not spelled out, but the general principles are clear: there are two offices (elder and deacon), the leaders of the local church work jointly, churches are interconnected (see Acts 15) and the people of God choose their leaders. The early church leaders used this pattern for church government when they established worshiping groups. And when John Calvin set about to reform the church in the 1500s, he felt the best way to proceed was to go back to the New Testament and structure the government of the church as it is found there.

Now look at the qualifications for church office. Paul first gives the qualifications for the office of elder (vss. 1–7). As we consider these, remember that they are the characteristics of a spiritually mature person, which should be the goal of all of us. So measure yourself by these benchmarks.

An elder must be "above reproach." Think of the damage done when a church leader lives in an immoral or dishonest way! An elder must be "the husband of but one wife." (Paul obviously taught that such officers were to be male.) The reference to one wife raises the question of whether experiencing a divorce would disqualify a person from serving. Commentators are divided on whether this refers to divorce or polygamy. Hendriksen says the meaning is that an elder "must be a man of unquestioned morality, one who is entirely true and faithful to his one and only wife." If the expression applies to divorce, we should ask whether the divorce was prior to the elder candidate's becoming a Christian or whether he had biblical grounds for his divorce (see Matt. 19:9 and 1 Cor. 7:15). In such a case he would be free to hold an office in the church. Otherwise you could create a set of circumstances in which *one person*—a murderer, for example—might become converted and in time could become a church officer, but *another person*—one who had been divorced (and could not remarry his first wife)—also might later became a believer, but could *not* hold church office.

A leader must be temperate in his lifestyle. He is to be self-controlled, not swayed by sudden impulse in his judgments, but steady and calm. He must be respectable, demonstrating the good behavior you would expect of a person of high moral character. And he should be a hospitable person, generous and concerned to meet the needs of others.

Another necessary quality is that an elder should be able to teach. Obviously there are different degrees of ability here, but all leaders should know their Bible and be able to apply the Word to differing situations with discernment.

An elder should not be "given to drunkenness" (vs. 3), which can be translated "one who lingers beside his wine." The Bible doesn't say it's a sin to drink, but it does warn of the danger of strong drink and also of the stumbling block this can be to others. If a person's drinking is a stumbling block to others, Paul urges that person to forego taking a drink (Rom. 14:21). I personally believe that in our current situation in America, it is far better for a church leader to abstain from drinking, but each individual must decide this before the Lord.

The elder is not to be a "violent" or quick-tempered person. A verse of Scripture that often comes to mind is that "everyone should be quick to listen, slow to speak and slow to become angry, for man's anger does not bring about the righteous life that God desires" (Jas. 1:19, 20). Likewise an elder shouldn't be a "quarrelsome" or contentious person; rather, he should be a peacemaker. Nor is an elder to be a lover of money or covetous. He must be free from materialism with its false value system.

Paul wants us to consider the households of potential leaders. An elder must "manage his own family well and see that his children obey him with proper respect" (vs. 4). Managing his own house is a good test of whether a man can manage God's church (vs. 5). He should not be a recent convert, which could lead to pride and great damage to himself and the church (vs. 6). His judgment and integrity should be respected by outsiders. If a person has a bad reputation in the community, that will hurt the church he helps to lead. As Hendriksen warns, the men who work with such a person will mock, "Have they actually made *you* an elder…*you?*" Moreover he himself may think, " 'If I can get away with this conduct of mine, and still be elected overseer, I can get away with anything.' Thus he will fall into the devil's *snare,* that is, into the devil's *trap,* hence, into his *power.*"[1]

The qualifications for the office of deacon (vss. 8–13) are similar to those for the office of elder. Deacons must be "worthy of respect," and they must be "sincere"—which means they should not speak out of both sides of their mouth. They must be free from addiction to alcohol and from pursuing material wealth dishonestly. They are to "keep hold of the deep truths of the faith with a clear conscience" (vs. 9). These truths are ones we wouldn't know unless God had revealed them in the Bible. Deacons must hold to these great truths of the Christian faith conscientiously, with a clear conscience, as they walk in the light, confessing and repenting of sin. Prospects for the office must "first be tested," demonstrating that they have maturity and faithfulness. People will recognize a good candidate as being blameless or above reproach.

In verse 11 Paul mentions the necessary qualifications for a third group, the wives of deacons or perhaps the women who assisted the deacons in their work (see Rom. 16:1, 2). (The Greek word referring to these women can be translated either way.) In either case such women are to be "worthy of respect, not malicious talkers but temperate and trustworthy in everything."

Paul returns to the qualifications of deacons in verse 12 and states that the family requirement for elders holds for deacons also: they are to be the husband of but one wife and manage their children and household well. He then speaks of the blessing that comes from rendering effective service as a deacon: "Those who have served well gain an excellent standing and great assurance in their faith in Christ Jesus" (vs. 13). This is a strong incentive to accept the responsibility of leadership in the church and to carry it out faithfully. We should look for men who come the closest to meeting this ideal pattern.

The Church's Role (3:14–16)

Paul tells Timothy that he is writing these things so that "you will know how people ought to conduct themselves in God's household, which is the church of the living God, the pillar and foundation of the truth" (3:15). Here we have the nature of the church's role—it is to be the pillar and foundation of the truth. The purpose of any "pillar and foundation" is to uphold, to be built upon. Calvin in *The Institutes of the Christian Religion* teaches that the first mark of the true church is faithfulness to the Word of God. Paul then lists the key elements in the truth that the church is to teach:

"Beyond all question, the mystery of godliness is great:

He appeared in a body,
    was vindicated by the Spirit,
was seen by angels,
    was preached among the nations,
was believed on in the world,
    was taken up in glory" (vs. 16).

Here is a summary of Christ's life from his birth to his ascension. (Paul may have been quoting a hymn of adoration to Christ.)

Being "vindicated by the Spirit" refers primarily to Christ's being raised from the dead. It was also especially at the resurrection that he was "seen by angels." After this, Jesus gave the Great Commission that resulted in his being "preached among the nations" and "believed on in the world." Finally he "was taken up in glory"—he ascended! Truly, great is the mystery of godliness. How crucial that the church fulfill her role as the pillar and foundation of the truth!

Our Part

As members of Christ's church we seek men for our leaders who have these qualifications. Perhaps you should seek to be such a leader yourself. Take the template for a church officer that Paul explains here, and put it up against your life. What corrections do you need to make? In a day when the church so desperately needs to be upholding the truth, why not desire the office of elder? Paul says, "Here is a trustworthy saying: If anyone sets his heart on being an overseer, he desires a noble task." (1 Tim. 3:1). It is commendable to seek leadership in the church for the right reasons. And how crucial it is that the church have good leaders!

Review Questions

1. What is the distinction in the New Testament between the offices of elder and deacon?

2. When Paul says to the elders of the Ephesian church that the Holy Spirit had made them overseers of that flock, what do you understand him to mean?

3. What incentive is there to want to serve as a leader in the church?

4. What, according to Calvin, is the first mark of the true church?

5. How should these qualifications for office be applied to an individual?

6

Teachers, True and False
1 Timothy 4:1–10

A few years ago the report of a liberal denomination's committee of ministers, academics and health professionals made headlines in most newspapers. In the report the committee assumes that sexual gratification is a human need and right that should not be limited to heterosexual spouses. Gays and lesbians are to "be received and accepted as full participant members" in the church and be eligible for ordination whether celibate or not. "What matters is not narrowly whether sexually active adults are married or not," the report claims, "but rather whether they embody justice-love in their relation." "Homosexual love, no less and no more than heterosexual love, is right and good."[1]

This report is just one manifestation of the grossly unbiblical teaching that appears in some churches today. In anticipation of this Paul warns about false teachers and calls on Timothy to be a true one. What's the difference? How can we avoid being led astray by the former, and how can we be, and know, the latter?

False Teachers (4:1–5)

Paul reminds Timothy that "the Spirit clearly says...in later times some will abandon the faith and follow deceiving spirits....Such teachings come through...liars" (vss. 1, 2). The later times or last days began at the first coming of Christ (see Acts 2:17; Heb. 1:1, 2). Six years earlier Paul had warned the elders of the Ephesian church: "Keep watch over yourselves and all the flock....I know that after I leave, savage wolves will come in among you and will not spare the flock. Even from your own number men will arise and distort the truth in order to draw away disciples after them" (Acts 20:28–30).

What was the character of this false teaching? In general it was an abandonment of—a departure from—the faith, from the body of redemptive truth that was "once for all entrusted to the saints" (Jude 3). These truths were normative. As Paul writes to the Galatian church, "But even if we or an angel from heaven should preach a gospel other than the one we preached to you, let him be eternally condemned" (Gal. 1:8).

Abandoning the truth has taken many forms from Paul's day to ours. In the early church, Judaizers erroneously taught that salvation comes, at least in part, by works. Paul denounced them saying, "You who are trying to be justified by law have been alienated from Christ; you have fallen away from grace" (Gal. 5:4).

In the early part of the fourth century, Arius taught falsely that Jesus was not fully divine. His position was that Jesus was a particularly splendid human being but not God the Son. This teaching became very popular, but Athanasius stood firmly for the full divinity of Christ. Eventually the church adopted the position of Athanasius at the Council of Chalcedon in A.D. 451 and asserted that Jesus is both true God and true man.

Also in the fourth century, Pelagius taught that people are not fallen and can keep the Ten Commandments through their own inherent abilities. Augustine opposed him with the biblical teaching about the fallen nature of human beings with its bias toward sin—original sin. Augustine pictured humankind as the man who was robbed and beaten in the parable of the good Samaritan; human beings need to be rescued by Christ. Semi-Pelagianism (which—like Arminianism today—didn't adequately acknowledge the effects of sin upon the human will) became entrenched in the church until Luther, Calvin and the other Reformers put that departure in its true light.

Early in the twentieth century, modernism questioned the necessity of Christ's atonement and its substitutionary nature. Modernists argued that since God is love, no atonement is needed; all we need to do is return as the prodigal son did to his father. More recently, universalism, the concept that all people will ultimately be saved, has become popular in many sections of the church. You will find universalism in many other places, too. For instance, in writing about the theology behind the comic strip Peanuts, Robert Short says,

> We have said that the Christian is finally distin-guished from the non-Christian by something the Christian *knows* about the finale of history: eter-nal salvation has already been made sure once for all time and for all men through Jesus Christ.[2]

Whatever form abandoning of the faith may take, it is wrong. Our job is not to refashion the gospel but to pro-claim it, trusting God to use it in remaking people.

The specific departure that Paul was referring to in his letter to Timothy involved extreme asceticism. The false teachers were forbidding people to marry and were order-ing them to abstain from certain foods (vs. 3). God does call some to the single life because of the kingdom of heaven (Matt. 19:12), but this is different from claiming that it is wrong to marry or that celibacy is a superior calling.

Paul answers this departure from the truth by arguing that God gave us the institution of marriage and different foods to eat, and both are "to be received with thanksgiv-ing." They are sanctified (consecrated, made holy) to us when we receive them as from God's hand and thank him for them. For everything created by God "is good, and noth-ing is to be rejected if it is received with thanksgiving" (vs. 4). (Note that Paul grounds his teaching on this matter in creation just as he did his teaching about the roles of men and women.) If God has not forbidden something in his

Word, Christians have freedom to do it or not do it as they see fit. They should be careful about causing others to stumble spiritually (Rom. 14:13), but the principle must be upheld that God alone is Lord of the conscience and his Word alone determines right and wrong. We must not add to or take away from the commandments of God.

What was the cause of the false teaching to which Paul was referring? Paul traces its origin first to deceiving spirits. He said these false teachers "follow deceiving spirits and things taught by demons" (vs. 1). Satan and his emissaries wage a bitter war against the truths of the gospel and seduce many even as Satan seduced Eve (see 2:14). (C. S. Lewis masterfully pictures the conflict in *The Screwtape Letters,* a book well worth reading.)

A second cause of the departure, however, was the silenced consciences of the false teachers, who were "hypocritical liars, whose consciences have been seared as with a hot iron" (vs. 2). These men had known better—their consciences told them they were doing wrong—but they went against conscience until it was cauterized and no longer spoke with authority. Hallesby, the author of a book on the conscience, says that there is an organic connection between the conscience and the will. The conscience addresses itself to the will; if the will accedes to the demand of the conscience, then the conscience grows stronger and speaks more accurately and authoritatively. But if the will refuses to yield, then gradual deadening of the conscience occurs. There begins to grow in us that deceitful nature that with devilish logic wards off every accusation of conscience:

If a person has employed deception...an awakening becomes almost an impossibility because deception leads to the...hardening of the heart (Eph. 4:18), or simply...a hardening (Rom. 11:7; see also Heb. 3:13, 15).

This condition represents the...definite death of conscience.

It is no longer possible to awaken such a conscience. [Therefore] such a person is eternally lost, for salvation cannot reach a person except through his conscience....

This condition is spoken of...as *blasphemy against the Spirit* (Matt. 12:31). The Bible says expressly that there is no forgiveness for this sin.

It does not consist in any sinful act, no matter how gross it may be, but is a condition of the conscience, one which is the result of a shorter or longer development.[3]

The True Teacher (4:6–10)

Paul tells Timothy how to be a true teacher and how to protect his flock from false teachers: "If you point these things out to the brothers, you will be a good minister of Christ Jesus, brought up in the truths of the faith and of the good teaching that you have followed" (vs. 6). "These things" refers to the great biblical truths Paul had taught and the warning concerning any abandoning of the faith. This kind of teacher engages in a continual process of nourishing himself and his flock in sound Christian doctrine. Timothy is well grounded in these truths. It is better to light a candle than curse the darkness. The best way to combat error is to teach the truth.

Timothy is to "have nothing to do with godless myths and old wives' tales" (vs. 7a). Apparently Paul is speaking of the "myths and endless genealogies" he had referred to earlier (1:4). These are not spiritually nourishing, and Timothy should not waste his time on them. Rather he should train himself to be godly (vs. 7b). The same applies to us if we are to be mature Christians and teachers.

Paul now compares the value of bodily exercise with spiritual discipline that results in spiritual growth. Physical exercise profits some, but "godliness has value for all things, holding promise for both the present life and the life to come" (vs. 8). Physical exercise is good for this life, godliness for both this life and the next!

What a difference it would make if people who are serious about maintaining their physical health gave the same concern to the well-being of their soul! What about you? Do you give as much time to staying in spiritual shape as you do to staying in physical shape? Do you show as much concern for your children's spiritual development as you do for their physical growth?

The purpose for which Paul was laboring was to let people all over the world hear of Christ and receive eternal life. "For this we labor and strive, that we have put our hope in the living God, who is the Savior of all men, and especially of those who believe" (vs. 10). The true teacher must labor and strive (Greek *agonizomai*), agonizing as he struggles against the forces that oppose the gospel—the hardness of people's hearts, the false teachers and, behind it all, deceiving spirits. As he does this, the true teacher must put his hope in the living God who, because he is alive, can empower his true teacher and can set before him open doors in spite of opposition (see 1 Cor. 16:9).

God is the "Savior of all men, and especially of those who believe," says Paul. God is not the Savior of all men in the sense in which the universalists teach; that is contrary to the teaching of the entire Bible. The phrase "especially of those who believe" indicates that Paul is using the word *Savior* in a twofold way. First, God is the Savior or preserver of all men in the sense that by his common grace he provides the sun and the rain for all, he gives "all men life and breath and everything else" (Acts 17:25). But in a higher sense God is the Savior of those who believe, those who embrace his Son by faith, because he gives them everlasting life in all its fullness!

Teaching Ourselves

These things are crucial to our well-being and the church's! In our day there is widespread departure from the gospel of Christ. How grounded are you in the apostles' teaching so that you are not led astray? How careful are you to maintain a good conscience? Samuel Rutherford said, "Fear your light, stand in awe of it, for it is from God. Kings cannot heal broken consciences." How dreadful to think of the degeneration and death of conscience.

Are you training yourself spiritually so that you become more godly? Do you understand how profitable that is for both this life and the next? What changes do you need to make in your life in order to do that? Are you striving, as Paul did, to make the gospel available to people everywhere so that they may receive everlasting life?

Review Questions

1. What is the criterion Paul gives to determine whether someone is teaching falsely?

2. What was the nature of the departure from sound teaching that Paul referred to in this section of his letter?

3. How does Paul answer the false teaching?

4   According to Paul, what causes such false teaching?

5   What should characterize a true teacher?

7

When You're a Young Leader
1 Timothy 4:11–5:2

Timothy, a young man about 35, was an apostolic representative dealing with all the elders of the churches of Ephesus and the surrounding area. These elders were generally older men, so Timothy could have felt awkward at times. Many young pastors find it touchy to relate to other elders who are much older. I recall a young minister who suggested to his board of elders (session) that they rotate members out of office periodically. One elder replied, "Young man, you don't understand. We rotate preachers!"

How then does a younger person lead effectively in the church in positions where he has been properly placed?

1. By Teaching Basic Principles (4:11)

Paul tells Timothy, "Command and teach these things."

What things did Paul have in mind? He is referring to the things he had been emphasizing, such as to beware of false teaching involving an unbiblical asceticism (vss. 1–5), to nourish oneself on words of faith and sound doctrine (vs. 6), to train for godly living (vss. 7, 8) and to teach that God is the Savior of all who believe (vs. 10). Certainly a key ingredient for leading in any type of ministry is making sure you are growing spiritually and then helping to establish other people in those same basic Christian truths and habits.

2. By Setting an Example (4:12)

Respect cannot be demanded; it must be earned. Paul tells Timothy, "Don't let anyone look down on you because you are young." Timothy must see to it that he is respected. But how? By being an example, says Paul, and winning people's respect! Paul mentions five areas for Timothy to address.

First, Timothy is to pay attention to the way he speaks to others. How damaging intemperate language, gossip, impure jokes and sarcasm can be! Paul says, "Do not let any unwholesome talk come out of your mouths, but only what is helpful for building others up" (Eph. 4:29). And the writer of Proverbs gave similar advice. "The tongue that brings healing is a tree of life" (Prov. 15:4).

The second area is behavior—Timothy's dealings with people, his habits, his lifestyle. How do you treat others, spend your money, dress, discipline yourself and handle your children?

A third area is love, a genuine concern for the welfare of others and a willingness to deny yourself for their sake. We need to live out the parable of the good Samaritan. If we love and serve the people we are trying to lead, soon they will be willing to follow us even in very difficult undertakings.

Fourth, is faith—a life of trusting God, looking to him to provide and protect. As Hudson Taylor said, "All God's giants have been ordinary men who accomplished great things because they reckoned on God's being with them."

Purity—conforming in thought, word and deed to God's moral law—is the fifth area that Paul mentions. Timothy should avoid lust, bitterness and lying. What a mine field this is for *any* leader today—particularly young ones!

3. By Being Devoted to Scripture (4:13)

Paul tells Timothy to pay attention to "the public reading of Scripture." The early church continued the synagogue practice of the public reading of God's Word (Luke 4:16) but included growing portions of the New Testament. Since there were very few copies of the Scriptures available, this was crucial. "Preaching" includes warning against error and encouraging and challenging people to step out in obedience and faith in many different areas. "Teaching" involves instruction in the basic doctrines of Scripture. As Timothy gave attention to reading, exhortation and doctrine, he was both exercising and establishing his authority and pointing his people to the ultimate authority. Young leaders gain proper recognition by demonstrating that they are yielded to the authority of God's Word and by urging their followers to do the same. As people gain confidence in their leader's ability to handle the Word and as the Word is assimilated into their lives, they willingly follow their young leader.

4. By Exercising Your Spiritual Gift (4:14)

Paul tells Timothy not to neglect his gift. He is referring to a spiritual gift (see 1 Cor. 12:1ff.) given to him by the Spirit of God. The gift is not identified, but it may have been teaching, prophecy, exhortation or all three. The gift equipped Timothy for the ministry to which God had called him, and he must not grow careless about developing and using it. Every Christian has at least one gift that the Holy Spirit has given for service. All Christians must discover and develop their gifts.

When a world-class athlete joined our church and tried to discover his gift, I suggested that he try our personal evangelism training. Later I suggested that he lead a small-group Bible study. Neither seemed to be the appropriate slot. One day he showed me an advertisement for a conference on the family in Kansas City. He said he thought he might attend and see what they had available to help local churches gear up to assist families. I said, "Wonderful!"

The young man returned after attending the conference and deposited a huge pile of literature on my desk saying, "It was great! You need to read this!"

I replied, "You were there. Why don't you read it and tell me what you think we ought to do?" Off he went with the material. A month later he came back and proposed that we offer an elective class on the family each quarter, using differing themes. He also suggested appropriate material. He recommended that we have an annual family-life conference and use speakers with special expertise in that area. "You know what we're going to do?" I said. "We're going to set up a committee, put you in charge of it and let you implement this!" Soon all was in place; he was fulfilled and fruitful, and the whole church was helped. What had happened? He started exercising his gift.

Timothy's gift was given "through a prophetic message when the body of elders laid their hands on" him (vs. 14). Paul's own hands had also rested on him (2 Tim. 1:6). This laying on of hands symbolized the conferring of such gifts by God, and often God actually conferred them on that very occasion (see Acts 8:17, 9:17). At the time when hands were laid on Timothy, a prophecy was given concerning the gift. Young leaders need to discover their gifts and labor primarily within the bounds of those gifts. They should carefully develop them by study, practice and learning from others with similar gifts. As they do, their leadership will be respected.

5. By Progressing Spiritually (4:15)

All of this required real commitment on Timothy's part. Paul writes, "Be diligent in these matters." "These matters" refers to that entire fourth chapter: beware of false teaching, nourish yourself on sound doctrine, discipline yourself for godly living, be an example in the areas mentioned and exercise your spiritual gift. Timothy was exhorted to give himself "wholly to them," being absorbed in them "so that everyone" could see his "progress." When people see young leaders progressing spiritually, they are encouraged and want to help them carry out the vision and work God has given them. People who are earnest about the things of God will be attracted to such leaders and will join hands with them.

6. By Being Consistent (4:16)

In summary Paul says, "Watch your life and doctrine closely. Persevere in them." Holy living and sound teaching must go together; neither can be neglected. As the Puritans used to say, "Truth is in order to godliness."

This requires vigilance and perseverance. Follow this path, and don't let anything divert you! Why? Because the stakes are so high! "Because if you do, you will save both yourself and your hearers." Conversely, if you go seriously astray, both you and those you teach will be damaged. We must never forget that there is a great battle going on for the souls of people! God will keep us when we belong to him, but one way he does this is to move us by such warnings.

7. By Guarding Your Relationships (5:1, 2)

Paul gives advice to Timothy on how a young leader should relate to various groups. First are the older men: "Do not rebuke an older man harshly, but exhort him as if he were your father." Sometimes a young leader has to correct someone older. (Since verse 2 refers to older women, verse 1 refers to older men, not the office of elder.) It is not appropriate for a young leader to sharply reprimand someone older. Yet the young leader must approach the older man and entreat him to change, showing him respect as he would his father. Humility is important in such an undertaking. Likewise, young leaders should treat older women as mothers. Finally, and most importantly, Timothy and other young male leaders are to guard their relationships with younger women, treating them "as sisters, with absolute purity." What a crucial area this is, and how essential it is to reflect on the possible consequences of failure to do this. One young leader says:

> Whenever I feel particularly vulnerable to sexual temptation, I find it helpful to review what effects my action could have:
>
> • Grieving the Lord who redeemed me.
>
> • Dragging his sacred name into the mud.
>
> • One day having to look Jesus, the Righteous Judge, in the face and give an account of my actions.
>
> • Following in the footsteps of those people whose immorality forfeited their ministries and caused me to shudder: (list names).
>
> • Inflicting untold hurt on Nanci, my best friend and loyal wife.
>
> • Losing Nanci's respect and trust.

- Hurting my beloved daughters, Karina and Angie.

- Destroying my example and credibility with my children, and nullifying both present and future efforts to teach them to obey God ("Why listen to a man who betrayed Mom and us?").

- If my blindness should continue or my wife be unable to forgive, perhaps losing my wife and my children forever.

- Causing shame to my family ("Why isn't Daddy a pastor anymore?").

- Losing self-respect.

- Creating a form of guilt awfully hard to shake. Even though God would forgive me, would I forgive myself?

- Forming memories and flashbacks that could plague future intimacy with my wife.

- Wasting years of ministry training and experience for a long time, maybe permanently.

- Forfeiting the effect of years of witnessing to my father and reinforcing his distrust for ministers that has only begun to soften by my example, but that would harden, perhaps permanently, because of my immorality.

- Undermining the faithful example and hard work of other Christians in our community.

- Bringing great pleasure to Satan, the enemy of God and all that is good.

- Heaping judgment and endless difficulty on the person with whom I committed adultery.

- Possibly bearing the physical consequences of such diseases as gonorrhea, syphilis, chlamydia, herpes and AIDS; perhaps infecting Nanci or, in the case of AIDS, even causing her death.

- Possibly causing pregnancy, with the personal and financial implications, including a lifelong reminder of my sin.

- Bringing shame and hurt to these fellow pastors and elders: (list names).

- Causing shame and hurt to these friends, especially those I've led to Christ and discipled: (list names).

- Invoking shame and lifelong embarrassment upon myself.[1]

Need I say more?

Review Questions

1. How can young leaders earn the respect of their elders?

2. What are some areas in which Paul challenges Timothy to be an example?

3. What is a spiritual gift? How do people ascertain their gift(s)?

4. When Paul tells Timothy to "watch your life and doctrine closely. Persevere in them, because if you do, you will save both yourself and your hearers," is he implying that Timothy could lose his salvation?

8

The Care and Nurture of Widows

1 Timothy 5:3–16

Paul's theme in this letter has been "how people ought to conduct themselves in God's household, which is the church of the living God" (3:15). Paul's concerns were wide in scope, and we will now look at more of them.

In the days of the early church, women had difficulty finding gainful employment, and there was no unemployment insurance program to fall back on. The demanding job of caring for widows had first come to light in the tension that erupted in the Jerusalem church over its failure to take care of Grecian widows (Acts 6:1–3).

Thus, Paul advises Timothy on the proper way to care for widows. In our day widows have some safeguards, such as social security; yet, for various reasons, many still find themselves destitute. And the family has experienced a breakdown to the point that one out of every two marriages ends in divorce. Consequently many women head households that can barely make it financially.

The Responsibility of the Church
to Care for Widows (5:3–7)

Paul says, "Give proper recognition to those widows who are really in need" (vs. 3). What recognition, or honor, is Paul talking about? It not only means to treat widows in the church with high regard but also to give them material support when they need it. It is the church's responsibility to look after them.

Paul lists the characteristics of the widow that the church should look after. She should be one who has no family to look after her. "Give proper recognition to those widows who are really in need. But if a widow has children or grandchildren, these should learn first of all to put their religion into practice by caring for their own family." Next, the widow the church should look after "puts her hope in God and continues night and day to pray and to ask God for help" (vs. 5)—she is a Christian widow. God encourages just such trust when he says, "Your widows too can trust in me" (Jer. 49:11).

In contrast Paul describes the widow who doesn't qualify for the church's help: "But the widow who lives for pleasure is dead even while she lives" (vs. 6). This widow is frivolous, showing by her behavior that she is spiritually dead. Paul teaches that "the mind of sinful man is death, but the mind controlled by the Spirit is life and peace" (Rom. 8:6).

The church is not obligated to help someone continue a sinful lifestyle.

It is important that Timothy give instructions about these things (vs. 7). He must see to it that the church gives "proper recognition" to genuinely dependent and deserving widows so that no one can blame the church for overlooking the needs of God's people.

The Responsibility of Relatives
to Care for Widows (5:4, 8, 16)

Paul tells believers they should help needy relatives who are widows (vs. 16). Sometimes children do not want to provide for a needy parent or grandparent. But Paul gives several reasons why relatives should look after their widows. First, true Christian living requires this (vs. 4). James says, "Religion...pure and faultless is this: to look after orphans and widows in their distress" (Jas. 1:27). The fifth commandment says we should honor our father and our mother, and certainly that honor shouldn't stop if they become needy!

Second, caring for widows enables children to repay their parents and grandparents (vs. 4) for all the love, effort and resources spent on them while they were being raised. It should be done with gladness and in a spirit of love.

Third, this is pleasing to God (vs. 4). God is a father and a defender of widows (Ps. 68:5), and he wants us to be the same. The next time you visit a widow, remember that you are demonstrating God's care for her.

Fourth, to fail to do this is to deny the faith, to bring

disrepute upon Christianity and to divert funds that are needed elsewhere to unnecessary areas. "If anyone does not provide for his relatives, and especially for his immediate family, he has denied the faith and is worse than an unbeliever" (vs. 8). Obviously this has wider application than just supporting widows—it applies to able-bodied persons working to provide for their household. If persons are able, but won't provide for their own, they have denied the faith by their actions. "Faith by itself, if it is not accompanied by action, is dead" (Jas. 2:17). Such neglect brings disrepute upon Christianity. Paul says persons who don't care for their needy relatives are worse than unbelievers. Even unbelievers often care for needy parents and work diligently to provide for their own. It is unthinkable that Christian morality should lag behind the world's standards!

When relatives fail to care for their widows, churches can find themselves diverting funds that are needed elsewhere into unnecessary areas. Relatives should help the widows in their families in order that the church not be "burdened with them, so that the church can help those widows who are really in need" (vs. 16). The church's funds are limited, and if it has to provide for some whose family could have provided for them, it means that the church may not have adequate funds to help others who have no families.

The Possibility of Widows
Rendering Special Service (5:9–15)

In verse 9 Paul speaks of a "list of widows." Apparently this was a group of godly widows to whom the church had given an appointed task as servants of the church. They possessed the necessary qualifications for the performance of certain spiritual and charitable functions. What were these special services? It seemed to have involved visiting the sick in their homes, counseling with the younger women (Titus 2:4, 5), possibly instructing children, and helping those in need. The church today always needs this type of ministry and certainly could benefit from the service of godly widows who perform such responsibilities. I think of how valuable the contribution of such women has been in my ministry through the years.

What were the requirements to be a member of this group of women? Such a widow had to be mature, at least 60 years old, and to have been faithful to her husband (vs. 9). (This couldn't mean that she didn't remarry earlier if her first husband had died when she was younger, since Paul encourages such remarriage in verse 14.) She should be known for her good deeds, such as bringing up children and showing hospitality. She should also have rendered humble service to fellow Christians, "washing the feet of the saints" and "helping those in trouble and devoting herself to all kinds of good deeds" (vs. 10).

Timothy should counsel the church not to put younger widows on such a list (vs. 11). Paul gives two reasons for this. First, it is unwise for younger widows to pledge not to remarry, and apparently such a commitment went with the position (vss. 11, 12). Should they later wish to marry, such an otherwise innocent desire would then be a rebellion against the yoke of Christ to which they had dedicated themselves. "Thus they bring judgment on themselves, because they have broken their first pledge" (vs. 12).

Second, the position would entail a special temptation to the younger widows to "get into the habit of being idle and going about from house to house" as well as being "gossips and busybodies, saying things they ought not to" (vs. 13). Older women would be less inclined to these temptations. In the light of this, Paul counsels that the younger widows should seek to remarry and raise children, be homemakers, and thus "give the enemy no opportunity for slander" (vs. 14). Paul doesn't identify the enemy, but obviously he has in mind any enemy of the cause of Christ. Our ultimate enemy is Satan, but his attack often comes through human agents. Paul knows of instances where some younger widows have already turned aside to follow Satan (vs. 15). This probably refers to giving themselves over to immoral living or being gossips and busybodies.

Applying These Principles Today

How does all this apply today? Having mature godly widows do special work in the church certainly seems like an excellent concept. They can give valuable counsel to younger women, can help greatly in the church's ministry to the afflicted and can be the backbone of the church's intercessory prayer ministry.

Currently there are not too many women in our congregations who fall into the category of young widows. Because of the high divorce rate, however, there are many single women who are heads of households. It would seem that

Paul's principles also apply here—that the church has the responsibility to help them. We should help with material support where needed but in other ways as well. They need help with their children. Possibly the church can implement a program to encourage two-parent families to "adopt" single-parent families, including them in various activities, such as recreation or picnics. This could provide a male role model for children. Qualified people in the church can help in many practical ways such as giving counsel in financial management, helping with home maintenance and assisting the family in moving.

A related principle would seem to be that young divorcées should remarry where there are biblical grounds for their divorces. Historically the church has recognized two such grounds: unfaithfulness (Matt. 19:9) and desertion (1 Cor. 7:15). The application of these grounds needs careful study, and books such as John Murray's *Divorce* and Jay Adams's *Marriage, Divorce and Remarriage in the Bible* are helpful.[1] The church should provide adequate counsel to divorcées and rejoice with them if they remarry. The temptation that besets the single-again group forms a background for some of Paul's counsel here, and the church would be wise to provide wholesome activities and programs for them.

Throughout Paul's teaching we can see the importance of the church's maintaining a good testimony for taking care of its own. To use Francis Schaeffer's phrase, the church is "always before the watching world." Therefore you must "let your light shine before men, that they may see your good deeds and praise your Father in heaven" (Matt. 5:16).

Several questions arise from our consideration. What is my church doing to meet the needs of widows or the single-again? What can I do personally? Is there a single-parent family I can help? Is there a widow or divorcée who is related to me whom I should be providing for? If you are a widow, do you have special experiences and abilities your church could use?

Review Questions

1. What kind of widow should the church provide for financially?

2. Why should relatives take care of widows instead of leaving it to the church?

3. How have persons who won't support their family denied the faith?

4. What were the qualifications for widows to serve in special ministries—visiting the sick, instructing other women, etc.?

9

How to Treat Your Elders

1 Timothy 5:17–25

How crucial it is that the church have good leadership! Paul again turns to the subject of elders in the church and how to treat them. His instruction is very pertinent to today's church and very practical. What shall we pay the preacher? What can we do about Elder Jones who is failing in his responsibilities? Do you think we should nominate Robert to the eldership? Paul gives principles that will help with such decisions.

The Distinction in the Remuneration of Elders (5:17, 18)

Paul makes a distinction among the elders (speaking now of the office) in terms of the work that they do and the way they do it. Some elders preach and teach. Presbyterian churches differentiate these *teaching elders,* or ministers, from *ruling elders* (see chapter five of this book). Paul also makes distinctions within the two groups by referring to some as those who "direct the affairs of the church well." Church members should acknowledge such men by counting them "worthy of double honor" (vs. 17). The position of elder should be held in honor in the church, and any who serve faithfully in the position should be honored. Those whose leadership excels, however, should be doubly honored, and this honor should especially go to those whose work is preaching and teaching.

"Honor" here carries (as did the same word in verse 3, there translated "proper recognition") the idea of material support. Not that every elder is to receive such support, but that those who spend a lot or all of their time in ministering should be paid. There is biblical warrant for such remuneration (vs. 18). Paul quotes both Deuteronomy 25:4 where God forbids muzzling the ox that treads out the grain and a saying of Jesus recorded in Luke 10:7, "The worker deserves his wages."

God has ordained that "those who preach the gospel should receive their living from the gospel" (1 Cor. 9:14). We know that Paul deplored leaders who were greedy (1 Tim. 3:3), but he equally deplored inadequate remuneration. Often, ministers and other salaried leaders are either overpaid or underpaid. Underpayment can lead to discouragement on the minister's part, resentment by his family, distraction from his work and a demeaning of the office. Overpayment can be a stumbling block to the congregation, leading them to lose the desire to give generously because they feel that the church is not spending its money well. Furthermore, the minister needs to model good stewardship and moderate living for his people.

Instruction about the Discipline of Elders (5:19–21)

If a church member decides to bring a charge against a teaching or ruling elder, the church should consider the accusation only if there are multiple witnesses to the offense (vs. 19). A church should not consider a charge when it lacks such support. This avoids damaging the reputation of a good leader.

If church members bring charges properly, however, and prove them to be true, the leader should be disciplined. "Those who sin are to be rebuked publicly" (vs. 20). Such disciplinary censure may require suspension or removal from office, suspension from the Lord's Supper or—as a last resort—excommunication (removal from the church—see 1 Cor. 5:13). The purpose of such public discipline (either before the elders or the congregation) is "so that the others may take warning." Discipline is always designed to bring an offender to repentance and restoration and to restrain others from bad behavior. Otherwise "a little yeast works through the whole batch of dough" (1 Cor. 5:6).

The church today has, in far too many instances, widely neglected the discipline of its leaders as well as the members of the congregation. Church discipline can, of course, be abused and can lead to a harsh spirit in a congregation or denomination. But neglect of it can also do great damage. Some of the most solemn meetings I have been in have involved the discipline of fellow ministers when they were suspended from the ministry. But some of the best meetings have been when suspended leaders repented and were restored to their office. Church discipline must, therefore, be done in a spirit of love, but it must be done.

The honor of Christ and his church are hurt when church leaders do wrong and the church does not discipline them. Think of the damage done to the church in the public eye when the state has to deal with those whom the church should have disciplined but didn't. Paul gives a solemn charge to Timothy "in the sight of God and Christ Jesus and the elect angels" to carry through on this (vs. 21). Apparently Paul was afraid Timothy might shrink back from such difficult matters and felt the need to admonish him.

The godly Scottish minister Robert Murray M'Cheyne said that the responsibility for exercising church discipline almost drove him from the ministry. No one is denying the agony involved in church discipline, but remember that you are in good company. The inclusion of angels in the charge reminds us that they are present at, and observing, church discipline and will be associated with Christ in the final judgment.

Paul warns that the church must carry out discipline without favoritism. The temptation is to go easy on the wealthy or influential leader or one with whom you are close friends. For instance, it's not uncommon to find churches with officers who are virtually inactive and yet are allowed to remain in office.

Caution in the Ordination of Elders (5:22, 24, 25)

Paul warns Timothy to prepare a man adequately before placing him as an officer in the church: "Do not be hasty in the laying on of hands" (vs. 22). The church can avoid much trouble if it follows the necessary precautions before ordaining men to office. Give men time and opportunity to develop and demonstrate their character, ability and knowledge. Are they humble? Do they walk in the light? Are they consistent? Do they serve faithfully, persevering at assigned tasks? Are they able to lead without lording it over others?

The church should evaluate men on the basis of all the qualities mentioned in 1 Timothy 3. Paul reasons that if Timothy participated in an ordination without a thorough investigation, he would share responsibility for the wrongs such elders might commit (vs. 22). Timothy must strive to keep himself pure, obeying God's Word with respect to this and all other matters. Paul emphasizes the importance of careful examination because, although some men's sins are obvious, "reaching the place of judgment ahead of them" (vs. 24), other men's are hidden and "trail behind them." Only a thorough examination of elder candidates will uncover anything that would exclude them from office.

The reference to judgment has to do with men's judgment before God after death. "Man is destined to die once, and after that to face judgment" (Heb. 9:27). Such a final judgment always forms the backdrop of a biblical world-and-life view. Furthermore, among godly men who are qualified for office there are those whose good deeds are obvious (vs. 25), but there are others whose good works are not so obvious and they might easily be overlooked. When the church gives careful examination, the good works of those men will not be hidden. If Timothy will exercise due caution and not be hasty in ordaining men to office, making sure they are trained, equipped and qualified, he will have good elders—and that will make all the difference!

The Medicinal Use of Wine (5:23)

Paul interjects a personal remark concerning Timothy's health: "Stop drinking only water, and use a little wine because of your stomach and your frequent illnesses." In Timothy's time water was often contaminated and could lead to sickness. Timothy's health was not good to begin with, so Paul advises using a little wine.

Timothy's ill health takes on significance in the ongoing debate over healing in the church today. Often people imply that if a person will exercise faith, he can claim healing. Such persons believe it is never God's will for a Christian to be sick. Interestingly, Paul doesn't tell Timothy to "claim his healing" but to use wine in a medicinal way.

A woman in my congregation developed breast cancer. After she had a mastectomy, a friend visited her in the hospital and said, "You know you didn't have to lose that breast, don't you?" How devastating and how misleading! We had prayed and asked for her healing, but it would have been a grave mistake to delay the operation and wait for healing.

Read the book *We Let Our Son Die* by Larry Parker.[1] They took their diabetic son off insulin, trusting God to heal him! That is not to say that God doesn't occasionally heal in an unusual way. But it is not his will to always heal, and failure to be healed doesn't necessarily indicate a lack of faith. Paul himself apparently suffered from some eye problem since he remarked to the Galatian Christians that they would have plucked out their own eyes and given them to him if possible (Gal. 4:15). Christians should use medical treatment, but at the same time they should ask God to heal with or without medicine according to his will.

Examining Our Practices and Our Lives

These matters are important! A church won't rise higher than its leaders. How do you select your officers? How do you develop leadership in your church? It is instructive to think of how Jesus developed leaders: he selected twelve men and poured his life into them. He trained them by teaching, by letting them observe his life and practice, by allowing them to participate with him in ministry, by stretching their faith and sending them out two by two to minister and then having them report back. Paul trained a similar team and could say to those among whom he ministered, "Whatever you have learned or received or heard from me, or seen in me—put it into practice" (Phil. 4:9). Formal training courses can help, but your most important tool in training others is your own life.

When I graduated from seminary, I started a church and gathered people in small groups for discipleship. Our church leaders came from those groups. We continue this practice in our congregation, and it generates a steady stream of leaders. Those already trained, train others.

Do you carefully screen those you select for office? Do you adequately train and prove them before you place them in positions of leadership? What kind of honor do you give your leaders? If there is remuneration, is it adequate? Is it excessive? What about your church's perspective on "divine healing"? With so many viewpoints being espoused in this area, are you grounded in what the Scriptures teach on this? What about your own life? Is it such that you would be qualified to lead? Are you taking opportunities to become qualified? Are there secret sins that you need to deal with before God through the power of his Spirit?

Review Questions

1. What distinctions does Paul make between elders?

2. How would Paul want you to treat your elders?

3. What are the purposes of church discipline?

4. Why is it important to exercise caution in placing men in the office of elder?

5. What are the implications of Paul's advice to Timothy to use a little wine for his stomach's sake?

10

Does It Pay to Serve God?
1 Timothy 6:1–10

Does it pay to serve God? Those who proclaim a health-and-wealth gospel on radio and TV today forcefully bring that question before us. They preach a message that health and prosperity are the rights of every Christian who will appropriate them through faith. God intends prosperity for all faithful believers, they claim, and only a lack of personal faith keeps them from experiencing it.

Asaph wrestled with this question in a different form in Psalm 73. As he looked around, he saw the prosperity of the wicked and compared that to his own situation of being plagued with problems all day and then waking up the next morning to the punishment of a new day. He wondered if it paid to serve God. In a similar way, Paul warns Timothy about false teachers "who think that godliness is a means to financial gain" (vs. 5). But first he takes up the issue of slavery.

How to Regard Those in Authority over Us (6:1, 2)

Paul addresses "all who are under the yoke of slavery" (vs. 1). Slavery was common in Paul's day. In fact, estimates put the population of Rome at about one-third slaves. Roman law allowed masters to be extremely cruel to their slaves. We are not slaves, but others do exercise authority over us, whether an employer, a board of directors, a teacher, or someone else. How should we who are Christians regard those in authority over us?

Paul first speaks to those who are under the authority of a non-Christian. They are to "consider their masters worthy of full respect, so that God's name and our teaching may not be slandered." It would have been unthinkable to discredit Christianity by encouraging a revolutionary effort to undermine the social structure of that day. The principles Paul urges would in time undermine slavery as lives were changed and consciences convicted.

For Christians under the authority of Christian masters, the equality enjoyed in church might breed contempt and lead some slaves to despise their masters (vs. 2). But Paul says that they should "serve them even better"—let the Christian relationship lead to wholehearted service rather than to resentment and laziness. They should do this "because those who benefit from their service are believers, and dear to them" (vs. 2).

If you have employees who are Christians, they should

be your best workers. If you as an employee have an employer who is a Christian, that person should be more considerate and fair to employees than other employers are. (In Colossians 4:1 Paul elaborates on this theme: "Masters, provide your slaves with what is right and fair, because you know that you also have a Master in heaven.") Paul challenges Timothy to teach these things and to urge them upon believers. The goal of the gospel is love from a pure heart (1 Tim. 1:5), so Paul teaches that employer-employee relationships should demonstrate that the gospel has taken root in our hearts.

How to Regard Someone
Who Deviates When Teaching Us (6:3-5)

Next, Paul gives instruction on how to regard teachers who stray from the truth. What kind of deviation does he have in mind? Paul describes these instructors as those who teach "false doctrines and [do] not agree to the sound instruction of our Lord Jesus Christ and to godly teaching" (vs. 3). Such teachers don't agree with wholesome or healing words that mend lives. "The sound instruction of our Lord Jesus Christ" could refer to a collection of the sayings of Jesus but probably is a general reference to Christian doctrine. The teachings of Jesus Christ are godly; they produce godliness in our lives as God through his Spirit applies these teachings to our minds and hearts.

Notice how Paul describes such a deviant teacher. He is proud or conceited; he thinks that he knows more than the Son of God! Suppose I were to say, "Jesus taught that he is the only way (John 14:6), but I say that if you are a good person, you can approach God whether or not you believe in Jesus." To do that would be the essence of pride! Moreover, such a teacher "understands nothing" says Paul. Paul says that such a teacher has "an unhealthy interest in controversies and quarrels about words that result in envy, strife, malicious talk, evil suspicions and constant friction between men of corrupt mind." Likewise, he has "been robbed of the truth," embracing and teaching falsehood. Finally, he is selfish and thinks that "godliness is a means to financial gain" (vss. 4, 5).

Kenneth Copeland, a proponent of the health-and-wealth gospel, explains Mark 10:29 this way: "Do you want a hundredfold return on your money? Give, and let God multiply it back to you."[1] In analyzing the health-and-wealth movement, D. R. McConnell explains, "The will of God is assumed to be synonymous with the self-indulgent will of man. The believer can rest assured that it is God's will to grant him 'whatever his li'l ol' heart desires.' "[2] One recipient of a letter that used such fund-raising tactics wrote back and said, "If it really works that way, you send the money to me, and God will give *you* one hundredfold!"

Some Scripture passages do encourage giving by promising blessings, even material blessings. But we have to handle them carefully. For example, 2 Corinthians 9:6 reads, "Remember this: Whoever sows sparingly will also reap sparingly, and whoever sows generously will also reap generously." Charles Hodge, in commenting on this verse, says,

The sentiment here expressed is the same as in Prov. 11:24, "There is that scattereth and yet increaseth; and there is that withholdeth more than is meet, but it tendeth to poverty." It is comprehended also in the wider truth taught in Gal. 6:7. Our Lord teaches the same doctrine, Luke 6:38, "Give and it shall be given unto you"…and often elsewhere. It is edifying to notice the difference between the divine wisdom and the wisdom of men. As the proper motive to acts of benevolence is a desire for the happiness of others and a regard to the will of God, human wisdom says it is wrong to appeal to any selfish motive. The wisdom of God, while teaching the entire [negating] of self, and requiring a man even to hate his own life when in conflict with the glory of God, tells all who thus deny themselves that they thereby most effectually promote their own interests. He that loses his life shall save it. He that does not seek his own, shall best secure his own. He that humbleth himself shall be exalted. There can, however, be no hypocrisy in this matter. It is not the man who pretends to deny himself, to humble himself, or to seek the good of others rather than his own, while he acts from a regard to self, who is to be thus rewarded. It is only those who sincerely [subordinate] themselves to others, who shall be preferred before them. We may thence learn that it is right to present to men the divinely ordained consequences of their actions as motives to control their conduct. It is right to tell men that obedience to God, devotion to his glory and the good of others, will effectually promote their own welfare.[3]

Contentment (6:6–10)

Finally, Paul discusses how we should regard the situation in which God places us, especially as it concerns money. Because money was a chief concern of the false teachers, he warns about some of its dangers and explains how to combat them. First, he speaks of the excellence of contentment (vss. 6–8). The practice of "godliness with contentment is great gain" (vs. 6). What is the nature of this contentment? "Soul-sufficiency" is a good translation (Hendriksen). This contentment is not based on our circumstances. The Puritan Jeremiah Burroughs wrote a book titled *The Rare Jewel of Christian Contentment* in which he defines such contentment as "that sweet, inward, quiet, gracious frame of spirit, which freely submits to and delights in God's wise and fatherly disposal in every condition."[4]

Paul writes to the church at Philippi, "I have learned to be content whatever the circumstances" (4:11). Like Paul, you can learn this when God puts you in a difficult circumstance and you apply your biblical convictions about how God controls all events, loves you and promises to work all things together for good (Rom. 8:28). Knowledge of what we have in Christ forms the basis for this contentment. If we are Christians through faith in Jesus Christ, then God is our Father. We are justified (declared not guilty), we are indwelt by the Spirit of God, Christ is our Shepherd and heaven is our destination! Thus we are very rich, or as Paul says, we have nothing and yet possess everything (2 Cor. 6:10). The song "A Child of the King" puts it well:

> A tent or a cottage, why should I care?
> They're building a palace for me over there!
> Though exiled from home, yet still I may sing:
> All glory to God, I'm a child of the King!

Knowledge of the transitory nature of earthly possessions also contributes to such contentedness: "For we brought nothing into the world, and we can take nothing out of it" (vs. 7). If a man had a million dollars for a day and then lost it all, would you consider him rich? Our lifetime is but a day compared with eternity. Remember Jesus' parable of the rich man and Lazarus (Luke 16:19–31)? The rich man lived in luxury, while Lazarus the beggar laid at his gate. They both died; Lazarus went to heaven, and the rich man went to hell. Who was rich? Lazarus was, with durable riches. What an error to call the other man rich!

The knowledge that God establishes our situation in life helps us to be content. Burrough's definition said that Christian contentment is that frame of spirit that "freely submits to and delights in God's wise and fatherly disposal in every condition." It's God's providence that assigns us our situation in life. "Who gave man his mouth? Who makes him deaf or mute? Who gives him sight or makes him blind? Is it not I, the LORD?" (Ex. 4:11).

The key is to get our eyes off secondary causes and realize that

> Things don't just happen to children of God.
> They are part of the great master plan.
> The troubles, the sorrows, the reverses, the rod,
> Are strokes of the great Sculptor's hand.[5]

Only when you realize this, can you trust God and freely submit to, and delight in, his wise and fatherly disposal. Fanny Crosby demonstrates the right attitude in her hymn "All the Way My Savior Leads Me":

> All the way my Savior leads me;
> What have I to ask beside?
> Can I doubt his tender mercy,
> Who through life has been my guide?
> Heav'nly peace, divinest comfort,
> Here by faith in him to dwell;
> For I know, whate'er befall me,
> Jesus doeth all things well.

These words were penned by a woman who as a child was blinded by a quack doctor who put the wrong ointment in her eyes.

John Paton served as a missionary to the New Hebrides. Shortly after his arrival, his young bride gave birth to a son and then died. Soon his son also died. John Paton knelt by their graves and claimed that land for God. He wrote that

> It was difficult to be resigned and left alone in

sorrowful circumstances, but feeling immovably
assured that my God and Father was too wise and
loving to err in anything that He does or permits,
I looked up to the Lord for help and struggled
on in His work.[6]

Such contentment is a duty, says Paul: "If we have food
and clothing, we will be content with that" (vs. 8).

According to the Shorter Catechism the Tenth Commandment requires "full contentment with our own condition, with a right and charitable frame of spirit toward
our neighbor, and all that is his." It is not wrong to want to
improve our situation, but dissatisfaction with God's provi-
sion is improper. If we can't improve our circumstances,
we need to accept them as from God's hand for our good.

Not surprisingly, Paul moves immediately in this section
to the evil of covetousness (vss. 9, 10). "People who want to
get rich fall into temptation and a trap and into many foolish and harmful desires that plunge men into ruin and
destruction" (vs. 9). Think of Balaam, Achan and Judas in
the Bible; they all made terrible decisions in order to gain
some riches. And

> Still as of old
> Men by themselves are priced—
> For thirty pieces Judas sold,
> Himself, not Christ.[7]

Paul digs into this topic more deeply: "For the love of
money is a root of all kinds of evil. Some people, eager for

money, have wandered from the faith and pierced themselves with many griefs" (vs. 10). John Owen, the Puritan theologian, defined covetousness as "an inordinate [improper] desire with endeavor after the enjoyment of more riches than we have, or than God is pleased to give unto us, proceeding from an undue evaluation of them or love unto them." Christian contentment cures covetousness. The cure comes when I am convinced that God established my situation.

Furthermore, I should be conscious of how much I do have. "Keep your lives free from the love of money and be content with what you have, because God has said, 'Never will I leave you; never will I forsake you' " (Heb. 13:5). Here the poorest Christian is raised to a position above all unbelievers in the world!

Finally, contentment reminds me how much I owe to Christ (see 2 Cor. 5:14, 15).

Conclusion

Christian, do you realize you are one of the richest people on earth? If you are, then learn to express your contentment like Henry F. Lyte does in "Praise My Soul, the King of Heaven":

> Praise my soul, the King of Heaven,
> To his feet your tribute bring;
> Ransomed, healed, restored, forgiven,
> Who, like me, his praise should sing?

Also, remember how you came to this position. The infinitely rich Son of God set aside his riches and made himself poor in order to enrich you! Reflect on that, and dedicate yourself to his service! If you are not a Christian, you should be discontented! One day all the things you strive after will be taken from you, and you will be discontented forever. Just like the rich man in Jesus' parable, you didn't take the opportunity to receive the riches Christ offers through faith in him. Why not seize that opportunity now?

Review Questions

1. How should we regard those in authority over us?

2. According to Paul, what are some things that characterize false teachers?

3. What is Christian contentment?

4. What principles are key to our experiencing Christian contentment?

5. What is covetousness, and what is its cure?

11

A Charge to a Man of God
1 Timothy 6:11–16, 20, 21

I suspect that most of us have been given a charge at some point in our life—perhaps when we were graduated, or commissioned, or married or ordained. Probably no charge was so solemn or important as the one Paul gives to Timothy. And this charge applies to all Christians. (We'll deal with verses 17–19 in chapter 12.)

The Striking Contrast (6:11a)

Remember that Paul had just finished speaking of those who desired to be rich and exposed themselves to "temptation and a trap and…many foolish and harmful desires that plunge men into ruin and destruction" (vs. 9). In a striking contrast he says to Timothy, "But you, man of God…" The expression "man of God" obviously refers to Christian leaders, but it can also apply to all mature Christians, the pool of people from whom Christian leaders are chosen. Paul uses this expression in his second letter to Timothy when he speaks of Scripture being useful for teaching, rebuking, correcting and training in righteousness "so that the man of God may be thoroughly equipped for every good work" (2 Tim. 3:16, 17). In contrast to those who seek their satisfaction in the world's offerings, Christians—as men and women of God—are to have a totally different approach. Paul sets forth the details of how Timothy and we are to live.

The Summarizing Commands (6:11b, 12)

Timothy is to flee certain things, pursue other things, and fight the good fight of the faith. He is to "flee from all this," which refers not just to the love of money, but to all the things Paul has warned about beginning at verse 3, such as false teaching, the love of controversy and argumentativeness. In contrast, he calls for Timothy to pursue "righteousness, godliness, faith, love, endurance and gentleness." *Righteousness* refers to wholehearted obedience to the law of God, which is summed up in the two great commandments to love God and your neighbor. *Godliness* refers to pious conduct as opposed to taking the things of God and his Word lightly. *Faith* orients us to live in harmony with the unseen realities of heaven—"we walk by faith and not by sight"—and to rely daily on God.

In 1 Corinthians 13 Paul breaks down *love* into its constituent parts: "Love is patient, love is kind. It does not envy, it does not boast, it is not proud. It is not rude, it is not self-seeking, it is not easily angered, it keeps no record of wrongs" (1 Cor. 13:4, 5). The parable of the good Samaritan illustrates how love behaves. The main character sacrificially helps a person in need, even though that individual is his natural enemy.

Endurance—or patience—refers to persevering under adverse circumstances. *Gentleness* characterizes people who turn the other cheek, not demanding their rights. Christ, "when they hurled their insults at him,…did not retaliate; when he suffered, he made no threats. Instead, he entrusted himself to him who judges justly" (1 Pet. 2:23).

Timothy must "fight the good fight of the faith" (vs. 12). True Christianity is indeed a fight. Matthew Henry notes that "those who will get to heaven must fight their way" there. We fight against the flesh, that law within our members that wars against our new nature. We fight against wrong desires to conform to the world, to indulge ourselves or to put others down. We fight against the world, non-Christian society with its allurements and threats to nonconformists. We fight against the devil's subtle ways and brutal attacks. This fight is one of faith. We fight by exercising a general faith in the truths of God's Word and a specific and personal faith in Jesus Christ as the Son of God who made atonement for our sins. We learn to rely on him for daily victory over temptation rather than battling in our own strength.

We fight as David fought Goliath. David used all of his own skill and ability, but he didn't rely on his skill and ability. He said, "You come against me with sword and spear and javelin, but I come against you in the name of the LORD Almighty" (1 Sam. 17:45).

We fight in view of the prize—eternal life. Paul says "take hold of" or "keep your grip on" (Phillips) eternal life. Nothing else is as important—for "what good will it be for a man if he gains the whole world, yet forfeits his soul" (Matt. 16:26).

Timothy had been called by God's Spirit, who made him alive spiritually so that he responded in repentance and faith. He had made a "good confession in the presence of many witnesses"—probably at his baptism. Having started well, he must now hold on to what he has so that no one will take his crown (see Rev. 3:11). The great truth of God's preserving his people does not lessen the crucial need for Christians to persevere. J. C. Ryle notes that

> *The certain perseverance of believers does not free them from the necessity of watching, praying, and using means, or make it needless to ply them with practical exhortations.* So far from this being the case, it is just by the use of means that God enables them to continue in the faith. He uses warnings and conditional promises as part of the machinery by which He insures their final safety.[1]

The Solemn Charge (6:13–16)

Paul gives his solemn charge to Timothy and as he does, he reminds him of two witnesses, God and Jesus Christ (vs. 13). God is the One who "gives life to everything." He bestows and preserves life; his providence is over all things. Christ Jesus made the good confession before Pontius Pilate, standing firm in the face of persecution and death. Timothy likewise is to be faithful.

The charge itself is "to keep this command" (vs. 14). Paul is referring to the fleeing from sin, pursuing of righteousness, fighting the good fight of the faith (vss. 11, 12) and to everything he said with respect to the ministry of the gospel and proper conduct in the church. Timothy must fulfill the charge with the utmost consecration—"without spot or blame" (vs. 14). He is to do this "until the appearing of our Lord Jesus Christ." God will return Christ to earth "in his own time" (vs. 15). The world may reject him now, but at Christ's return "every knee [will] bow...and every tongue confess that Jesus Christ is Lord to the glory of God the Father" (Phil. 2:10, 11). God will openly manifest his own majesty and power as "the blessed and only Ruler, the King of kings and Lord of lords" (vs. 15).

After Paul speaks of God's sovereignty, he proceeds to describe God as the only one who possesses immortality (vs. 16). While "the believer *has received* immortality, as one receives a drink of water from a fountain," only God *possesses* it as the Fountain himself (Hendriksen). Paul describes God's transcendence—he "lives in unapproachable light"—and his invisibility—"whom no one has seen or can see." Obviously such a Being deserves our reverence, and Paul expresses his desire that God receive honor and demonstrate his might forever.

The Sacred Commitment (6:20, 21)

Finally, Paul charges Timothy to "guard what has been

entrusted" to his care, turning away "from godless chatter and the opposing ideas of what is falsely called knowledge" (vs. 20). Paul says that, first and foremost, Timothy should guard God's redemptive truth, the gospel of Jesus Christ. The core of Paul's message is that anyone who lives in rebellion against God is doomed to a horrible eternity unless he gets right with God. But God loves the sinner in spite of his sin and sent his Son to take that guilt upon himself. Any sinner who hears this news, repents of sin and submits to God by placing trust in Jesus Christ, will be freely, fully and forever forgiven and will become a child of God. God through Paul entrusted this amazing truth to Timothy and to us. Paul's directions are to guard it, defend it and protect it. It's like a precious wonder drug that has been entrusted to us; we must not tamper with it, or it will lose its curative qualities. Dispense it intact to a sick and dying world.

How is Timothy to do this? Paul warns Timothy to carefully avoid "the opposing ideas of what is falsely called knowledge." The first reason for steering clear of such speculative theories is the danger to his own soul. Some have professed these opposing ideas and in so doing "have wandered from the faith" (vs. 21). Paul might also have continued, "Some men started out similar to you, Timothy, preaching the truth, and then they began to accommodate the truth to those speculative theories. The first thing you know they had [as Phillips later said] 'lost their faith.' "

Henry Van Dyke in *The Lost Word* describes the tragedy. A father speaking to his son who had gone astray says, "My son, you have sinned deeper than you know. The word with which you parted so lightly is the key word of all life and joy and peace. Without it the world has no meaning, existence no rest and death no refuge."[2]

The second danger is losing the truth. One reason we have the truth today is because martyrs' hands have passed it on to succeeding generations. We must pass it on just as we received it!

The Searching Challenge

The secret to fulfilling the challenge, of course, is to be a man or woman of God, to maintain a wholehearted commitment to Jesus Christ. You must flee worldly things, follow after righteousness and fight the good fight of the faith. Are you doing that? Are you fleeing a materialistic approach to life, or do your standards mirror society's? Are you obeying God's moral law? Is your faith overcoming the world, the flesh and the devil? Are you guarding the precious deposit and spreading the true gospel with all of its uncompromising claims and demands?

> Fight the good fight with all thy might;
> Christ is thy strength, and Christ thy right:
> Lay hold on life, and it shall be
> Thy joy and crown eternally.
> Run the straight race through God's good grace,
> Lift up thine eyes, and seek his face;
> Life with its way before us lies,
> Christ is the path, and Christ the prize.[3]

Review Questions

1. Define and illustrate each of the virtues Timothy and you are to pursue (vs. 11).

2. Who or what are your spiritual enemies, and how do you fight them?

3. How does David's approach to fighting Goliath illustrate principles involved in the fight of faith?

4. How does the instruction to keep your grip on eternal life fit together with God's promise to keep his own people safe (see John 10:28 and Rom. 8:35–39)?

5. Why is Timothy to be so careful to guard or keep that which was entrusted to his care (vs. 20)?

CHAPTER

12

Using Riches Properly
1 Timothy 6:17–19

When author Pat Morton spoke to a group in our city, he posed this question: "If Jesus had $40,000 and knew of the starving people in Haiti, what kind of a car would he buy?" That question calls for some sober thinking.

Paul charges Timothy to challenge people about how they handle their material resources because this is a vital part of spiritual growth. Christians do not automatically know what God expects, and even when they do know, they need to be exhorted and encouraged to do what is right. Moreover, they need to hear about the promises of God that relate to using money. We live in a materialistic society whose values and practices we easily absorb into our thinking. But as the Spirit of God uses the Scriptures to constantly renew our minds, he keeps us from being conformed to the world (see Romans 12:2).

To Whom Is This Charge Addressed? (6:17a)

Paul tells Timothy, "Command those who are rich in this present world." What is meant by "rich"? Paul had just written that we should be content with food and clothing (vs. 8). Perhaps a reasonable definition of riches would be what is left over after our essential needs have been met. (Of course, we often feel we need things that we really don't.)

While some of us struggle to satisfy what we consider our essential needs, when we compare our situation to the rest of the world, we are all rich! You have doubtless seen the statistics: if you could reduce the world to a global village of 100 persons, 1 would have a college education, 50 would be suffering from malnutrition, 80 would live in housing unfit for human habitation and 6 would control half of the money of the entire village. So the charge is addressed to us—we are rich!

The Temptations We Are to Resist (6:17b)

Earlier Paul warned of the temptation of wanting to become rich (vss. 9, 10), but now he warns of temptations that beset those who *are rich*. First, there is the temptation to pride: "Command those...not to be arrogant." Pride is being impressed with myself. Money fuels pride; I can easily convince myself that I earned it, I deserve it and therefore I have a right to dispose of it as I wish.

Scripture cuts through that attitude by reminding us that everything in this life is on loan—each moment is dependent on God's mercy. Scripture also asks, "For who makes you different from anyone else? What do you have that you did not receive?" (1 Cor. 4:7) If we evaluate people by their material possessions, we would have to say that people like the apostle Paul don't count for much! Jesus said that "a man's life does not consist in the abundance of his possessions" (Luke 12:15).

Second, there is the temptation to trust in our wealth. Proverbs says, "The wealth of the rich is their fortified city" (Prov. 10:15). If we trust in our investments, or insurance (which we should carry) or even our jobs, we can be guilty of pride. This is inadequate security; Paul calls it "wealth, which is so uncertain." It can be removed overnight! Instead, we are to put our hope in God because he is our security.

But how do we do this? We start by trusting Christ as our Savior. Then we need to obey God in financial matters, trusting him to meet our needs. "But seek first his kingdom and his righteousness, and all these things will be given to you as well" (Matt. 6:33). Paul says that God "richly provides us with everything for our enjoyment." Thus the Bible doesn't teach asceticism, but it does teach moderation as opposed to indulgence or luxury. We shouldn't take as our standard the lifestyles of those around us.

Ronald Wallace, in summing up Calvin's teaching on stewardship, says moderation is

> an essential element in the ordered Christian life....A Christian...should live in a "sober and

frugal manner,"…curbing luxury and cutting out all show of superfluous abundance.…A rich man [may] live on a higher standard than the poor.…[But the] rich man is always being tested…[and must] learn to "use his abundance by preferring abstinence in the midst of plenty." Moderation is the best nurse of love.[1]

How to Use Wealth (6:18)

In general, Timothy is to charge those with material resources to use them to "do good." William Law in his classic *A Serious Call to a Devout and Holy Life* writes:

Another great reason for devoting all our estate to right uses, is this, because it is capable of being used to the most excellent purposes, and is so great a means of doing good. If we waste it, we don't waste a trifle that signifies little, but we waste that which might be made as eyes to the blind, as a husband to the widow, as a father to the orphan. We waste that which not only enables us to minister worldly comforts to those that are in distress, but that which might purchase for ourselves everlasting treasures in heaven. So that if we part with our money in foolish ways, we part with a great power of comforting our fellow creatures and of making ourselves forever blessed.…

If a man had eyes and hands and feet that he could give to those that wanted them, if he should either lock them up in a chest or please himself with some needless or ridiculous use of them instead of giving them to his brothers that were blind and lame, would we not justly reckon him as an inhuman wretch? If he should rather choose to amuse himself with furnishing his house with those things than to entitle himself to an eternal reward by giving them to those that wanted eyes and hands, might we not justly reckon him mad?

Now money has very much the nature of eyes and feet; if we either lock it up in chests, or waste it in needless and ridiculous expenses upon ourselves while the poor and the distressed want it for their necessary uses, if we consume it in the ridiculous ornaments of apparel while others are starving in nakedness, we are not far from the cruelty of him that chooses rather to adorn his house with the hands and eyes than to give them to those that want them....

If we waste our money, we are not only guilty of wasting a talent which God has given us, we are not only guilty of making that useless which is so powerful a means of doing good, but we do ourselves this further harm, that we turn this useful talent into a powerful means of corrupting ourselves; because so far as it is spent wrong, so far it is spent in the support of some wrong temper, in gratifying some vain and unreasonable desires, in conforming to those fashions and pride of the world, which as Christians and reasonable men we are obliged to renounce....

For so much as is spent in the vanity of dress may be reckoned so much laid out to fix vanity in our minds. So much as is laid out for idleness and indulgence may be reckoned so much given to render our hearts dull and sensual.[2]

Specifically, those with material resources are "to be rich in good deeds, and to be generous and willing to share" (vs. 18). Timothy must urge the rich to help others in need. God does not evaluate our giving by the amount we give but by our ability to give. Jesus said the widow gave more than all the rich because she gave out of her poverty, whereas they gave out of their wealth (Mark 12:44). God compares what we give to what we use for entertainment, clothes, furniture, stereos and cars. We must have an attitude that prepares us to distribute, "to be generous and willing to share." Calvin notes that while we are not commanded to literally give away all our goods, neither are we to give only what we can easily spare.

The Reason for Being Generous (6:19)

Paul now gives strong reasons for following through generously. First, we are laying up a treasure: "In this way they will lay up treasure for themselves as a firm foundation for the coming age." Everybody is interested in good investments. Jesus said, "Do not store up for yourselves treasures on earth, where moth and rust destroy, and where thieves break in and steal. But store up for yourselves treasures in heaven" (Matt. 6:19, 20). Gifts can be some of those good investments. Jesus told the rich young man, "Sell your possessions and give to the poor, and you will have treasure in heaven. Then come, follow me" (Matt. 19:21).

You may have heard the story about a lady who died and went to heaven. An angel was escorting her to her home there. As they went down a street, there was a lovely home on the right. She said, "Who lives there?"

The angel replied, "Your former grocer, Mr. Jones."

"Really?"

A beautiful home appeared on the left. "Your former hairdresser lives there."

The lady thought, "My goodness, no telling what kind of mansion *I'll* have!"

The angel came to a little shack and said, "This is it." The lady was crestfallen, so the angel explained, "We did the best we could with the material you sent up."

This treasure laid up will be acknowledged on the judgment day when Jesus says, "Come, you who are blessed… take your inheritance, the kingdom prepared for you….For I was hungry, and you gave me something to eat…I needed clothes and you clothed me…" (Matt. 25:34–36). We don't go to heaven because of our good deeds; salvation is by grace through faith, not by works (Eph. 2:8, 9). But Scripture explains that judgment includes works because true faith evidences itself in good works. Moreover, Christians will be rewarded in heaven to the degree that they practiced such works (see 1 Cor. 3:11–15).

Second, Paul tells us that those who share "take hold of the life that is truly life" (vs. 19). He speaks of life in the highest sense—spiritual life. Paul exhorts us to deal with our earthly resources in the prescribed way so that we may grip the spiritual side of life firmly. Remember Paul's warning: "The love of money is a root of all kinds of evil. Some people, eager for money, have wandered from the faith" (vs. 10). Generosity tames our lusts and provides an antidote to such temptations.

The Application to Our Lives

Ask yourself some searching questions about how you are doing in this area. Is your attitude toward your resources, "These are mine"? Or can you say, "These are God's things, and I am his steward. I will manage them for his glory and the good of my neighbor"? For a lot of us, one of the most important influences shaping our character is the attitude we take toward getting and distributing our wealth. Now is the time to help others; now is the time to invest that treasure wisely; now is the time to get a firm grip on real life; now is the time to tame that wrong desire!

Let me share a little of my personal experience. After I had been in seminary a year and was pastoring a church on the weekends, I began to wonder, *Am I a Christian? What is a Christian?* And I didn't know! Nor did I feel like asking anyone; after all, I was the preacher! As I studied the New Testament, I concluded that the key to being a Christian was to "believe on the Lord Jesus Christ," but I wasn't sure what that meant. Did it mean to believe that he is the Son of God who died for my sins? If so, I believed in him. But I wasn't sure that was all that it meant.

I met an Air Force chaplain with whom I felt free to talk, and so I asked him. He gave me a pamphlet that explained that believing in Christ didn't just mean believing about him but included placing my trust in him to save me. My reaction was, "That's too easy. That would be a gift!"

Meanwhile I came across Romans 6:23: "The wages of sin is death, but the gift of God is eternal life in Christ Jesus our Lord." I realized that salvation *was a gift* and that I had enrolled in seminary with the idea that "I've been so bad, that if I'm going to get to heaven, I'll have to be a preacher!" Now I realized I was not a Christian but had been trusting in my improved record. I transferred my trust to Christ alone. I was amazed at grace! Moreover I was grateful, and I wanted to express my gratitude.

It occurred to me to express my gratitude to God by increasing the percentage of my giving to the church each year. It wasn't hard—I was single, on the GI bill, pastoring a church on the weekends and flying in the Naval Air Reserves. So I just increased the percentage up from the 10 percent that I had been giving.

Then I got out of seminary, accepted a call to plant a church at a salary of $300 per month, got married and had three children in two and a half years! The church increased my salary when I got married and had children, and I wanted to increase the percentage of my giving. My wife was unpersuaded. "This is ridiculous!" she exclaimed. "There is no way you can give like you want to give, and have children. You've got to make a choice!"

Our third child was due soon, and my car was in shambles. "The baby is due in April, and the last one cost $500 just to get her out the hospital!" my wife reminded me. I just prayed, and when it came time to make the commitment, she was willing to increase the percentage—but with many prophecies of financial doom!

Soon a car dealer got converted and joined the church. I was discipling him, meeting weekly with him for lunch. As we were eating one day, my friend said, "I'd like to furnish you with a car. At the end of the year, turn it in, and I'll furnish you with another new car. Also, I'll fix your car up, sell it and give you the money. What do you think?"

I said, "That would be nice!" Later that day I drove home in a brand-new station wagon.

The next month, while my wife was in the hospital recuperating from giving birth, the car dealer phoned me and said, "I just sold your car. Drop by, and I'll give you the money." It was $500! I went to pay for the baby, only this was a $300 baby—a cheaper baby! I never did understand why our third child was less expensive, but we had a new car, a new baby and $200! My wife exclaimed, "The Lord did that!"

"Yes!" I responded. The next year she wanted to pledge everything we had. I said, "Wait a minute!"

We've tried to maintain an approach over the years of stretching ourselves, trusting God and seeing what he would do. This has been one of the most exciting aspects of the Christian life for us! It's also been interesting to watch our children grow up and adopt similar values and approaches to giving. And that is priceless to me! I know how important it is that we "take hold of the life that is truly life!"

Review Questions

1. How should you understand the term *rich* (vs. 17)? How rich can a Christian properly become?

2. What does the phrase, God "richly provides us with everything for our enjoyment" (vs. 17) imply about your lifestyle?

3. What does this passage say are some of the temptations that you must particularly guard against? How can you best do that?

4. What motivation for giving does Paul urge you to adopt in verse 19 (see various translations)? Does this teach salvation by works (see Matt. 6:19–21 and 1 Cor. 3:10–15)?

13

Wrapping It Up

Paul's letter to his young friend and associate Timothy deals with how people should conduct themselves in the household of God (3:15). The themes have varied widely—from how Timothy was entrusted with the gospel to the Christian management of material resources, from the qualifications for leadership to how to handle false teachers. But every topic is related to the issues we struggle with today as we seek to maintain the health of the church.

What could be more important than to maintain the gospel and disseminate it in an uncorrupted form or that the church be led by qualified individuals? In this chapter we'll briefly review material from the previous chapters so that we can better retain the content and feel the impact of the book as a whole.

Chapter 1: *The Goal of the Gospel* (1:1–10)

Paul addresses Timothy as his "son in the faith" and reminds him that he had left him in Ephesus to charge certain ones that they should no longer "teach false doctrines." The goal of the gospel is love out of a purified heart. The design of the Christian faith is to make us lovers of God and of fellow human beings. Some people in Ephesus had turned aside from that goal and, failing to understand the proper use of God's law, were teaching it incorrectly.

The proper use of God's law is to restrain our wickedness, to reveal our guilt and to be a rule for living. The gospel should make us obedient followers of Christ who seek to live daily by the Ten Commandments in the power of the Spirit and who are quick to repent when they fail. Christ died to accomplish that, and it should be our personal goal. Is this a priority in your life? This kind of living grows out of the ground of a purified heart, a good conscience and a sincere faith. Does that describe you?

Chapter 2: *Entrusted with the Good News* (1:11–20)

We raised the question, "What is the most precious thing ever committed to your trust?" Paul spoke of being entrusted with "the glorious gospel of the blessed God." Remember he had been a blasphemer and persecutor of the church, but Christ stopped him in his tracks, converted him and entrusted to him the good news that Christ came into the world to save sinners by dying for their sins.

Being entrusted with the gospel obligated Paul to preserve the gospel undiluted and to propagate it. It is like being entrusted with a cure for a deadly disease! Paul passed this trust on to Timothy, whom he encourages to endure by fighting the good fight and holding on to faith and a good conscience. The church inherited this trust. Are you compromising the message or your conscience? Are you spreading the message?

Chapter 3: *Shhh! They're Praying* (2:1–8)

Paul exhorts believers to pray for all people, especially government authorities. There is a connection between such praying and the conversion of people throughout the world. Good government promotes peaceful conditions that lead to favorable circumstances for the spread of the gospel.

God desires all men to be saved. There is one mediator, who gave himself a ransom for all. Paul sees the great doctrine of the substitutionary atonement as the heart of the gospel.

The conditions of effective prayer require that men hold up "holy hands…, without anger or disputing." A Christian must live in obedience and be asking in faith. What place does prayer hold in your life? If you are a man, are you taking the lead to incorporate serious prayer in your church and home?

Chapter 4: *What's a Woman to Do?* (2:9–15)

The place of women in church provokes much controversy today. Paul writes, "I do not permit a woman to teach or to have authority over a man" (vs. 12). The issue is not whether women are competent to teach, but how they do so in their relationship to the men of the church, who bear the primary responsibility for teaching and leadership. The Scriptures don't permit women to hold the office of pastor or elder or an equivalent position.

Some argue that Paul taught this in order to accommodate to the culture of his day, but if he were writing today, he would state it differently. Paul grounds his teaching, however, not in culture but in God's order of creation (vs. 13). To say that this contradicts Paul's statement that in Christ there is neither male nor female (Gal. 3:28) sets Paul against Paul and undermines the inspiration of Scripture.

On the other hand, there are abundant opportunities for women to serve in the church. If you are a woman, are you chafing under the biblical teaching that men should lead in the church, or are you encouraging men to lead and then seizing the many ministry opportunities available to you? If you are a man, are you assuming the responsibilities of leadership?

Chapter 5: *Who's Qualified to Lead?* (3:1–16)

Paul explains the qualifications for church officers. The qualities provide good benchmarks for all Christians to judge themselves by because they are measures of a spiritually mature person.

We usually refer to the elders "whose work is preaching and teaching" (5:17) as ministers; others we often call ruling elders. Deacons handle the distribution of gifts in the church's ministry of mercy.

Here Paul states the purpose of his letter: "You will know

how people ought to conduct themselves in God's household, which is the church of the living God, the pillar and foundation of the truth" (3:15). How crucial that the church has good leaders! Take the pattern or template of a mature Christian that Paul lays out, and place it up against your own life. What corrections do you need to make?

Paul also gives us a great summary of Christ's life from birth to ascension in what possibly were the words of an early hymn.

Chapter 6: *Teachers, True and False* (4:1–10)

Paul warns about false teachers and describes their instruction as an abandonment of the faith (4:1), the body of redemptive truth. (When Paul wrote to Timothy, the church already possessed a collection of normative teachings.) He particularly mentions false asceticism: "They forbid people to marry and order them to abstain from certain foods." Paul traces the cause of such false teaching to deceiving spirits and silenced consciences.

Paul then tells Timothy that to be a true teacher he must nourish himself in the truths of the faith and sound doctrine, and discipline himself for godliness. He instructs Timothy in how to protect his flock.

Chapter 7: *When You're a Young Leader* (4:11–5:2)

How does a young leader serve effectively? To help meet the challenge that Timothy faced, Paul lays out some key principles. Timothy should lead by following basic practices, such as being alert to false teaching, nourishing himself in sound doctrine and disciplining himself for godly living. Then he can be an example in speech and conduct, especially faith, love and purity.

A leader needs to have Scripture as a foundation, and labor in the area of his spiritual gifts. As people see a leader's own spiritual progress and consistency, the flock will gain confidence in his leadership.

Finally, the young leader must guard his relationships, relating properly to different groups, especially being careful to relate to younger women "as sisters, with absolute purity."

Chapter 8: *The Care and Nurture of Widows* (5:3–16)

Paul points out that the church should care responsibly for widows in the congregation who have no other means of support. If the widow has a family, the responsibility for her care rests on them, and they should shoulder it so the church can use its resources to help those who have no families. Family members who are able to do this, but refuse to do so, deny the faith and bring disrepute upon Christianity.

In the early church a group of older widows were appointed as servants of the church. They probably visited the sick, counseled younger women, taught children and did other charitable works. Such a position for godly widows in the church today would be beneficial.

Paul tells younger widows to remarry and raise children. We suggested that this principle of the church's responsibility to care for widows could be applied today to the large number of single women who are heads of households.

What is your church doing to meet the needs of widows or single parents? What can you do personally?

Chapter 9: *How to Treat Your Elders* (5:17–25)

How crucial that the church have good leadership! Paul discusses the remuneration of teaching elders or ministers and how any elder should or should not be disciplined.

Paul warns Timothy to be cautious in the ordination of elders: "Do not be hasty in the laying on of hands." Men should be tested first, demonstrating over an appropriate period of time the necessary character and abilities to lead. We develop leaders best as Jesus trained his, by small-group discipleship. Are you willing to serve as a leader?

Paul gives a personal word of advice to Timothy: "Use a little wine because of your stomach and your frequent illnesses." This is related to the weighty question of "divine healing." Timothy was to use wine in a medicinal way, not just lay claim to healing. Shouldn't we pray for God to heal with or without means? Do you have sound biblical views in this important area?

Chapter 10: *Does It Pay to Serve God?* (6:1–10)

Paul discusses how to regard teachers who deviate from "the sound instruction of our Lord Jesus Christ." Such false teachers are conceited, delight in controversy, are selfish and suppose that "godliness is a means to financial gain" (6:5).

This speaks directly to today's health-and-wealth gospel. While some Scripture passages do encourage us to give, and promise material blessings, it is necessary that our motives be correct.

When Paul also tells us "godliness with contentment is great gain," he encourages us to seek Christian contentment and avoid the evil of covetousness. What is your view of whether it pays to serve God? What is your motive in giving? Are you experiencing the "rare jewel of Christian contentment"?

Chapter 11: *A Charge to a Man of God* (6:11–16, 20, 21)

Paul ends with a solemn charge to Timothy: "But you, man of God, flee from all this." He is to flee the love of money, false teaching and argumentativeness, and to follow after righteousness, godliness, faith, love, endurance and gentleness. And he is to fight the good fight of the faith, facing off against the world, the flesh and the devil through faith.

The prize is eternal life, and Paul says to "take hold of" or "keep your grip on" it. God will keep us, but we are to persevere. Timothy is to do this "until the appearing of our Lord Jesus Christ." Are you fleeing the love of money, following after righteousness and fighting the good fight of the faith?

Chapter 12: *Using Riches Properly* (6:17–19)

Paul urges Timothy to teach people how they should handle their material resources. There is a sense in which we are rich compared to the majority of people in the world. This can lead to pride and to trusting in our material resources instead of in God.

But Paul calls for moderation, not asceticism. Our money can be like eyes and feet to the poor, so we must not waste it. If we have material resources, we are "to be rich in good deeds, and to be generous and willing to share." As we do this, we lay up treasure in heaven that will be a good foundation on the judgment day. (This does not mean that we earn our salvation by good deeds.) It is thus that we "take hold of the life that is truly life"—grip the spiritual side of life firmly.

Are you managing your material resources as a steward or as an owner? Which word would better characterize your lifestyle, *moderation* or *indulgence?* What steps do you need to take in this area?

Chapter 13: *Wrapping It Up*

Review Questions

1. What is the primary theme of 1 Timothy?

2. What are some of the practical topics that Paul deals with in 1 Timothy?

3. What is the goal of the gospel?

4. What is Christian contentment and how can you have it?

5. How are the rich to regard their riches?

APPENDIX

THE MINISTRY OF THE CHURCH[1]

(It will be helpful to refer to the diagram on
page 153 while reading this appendix.)

The teaching of the Bible about the church constantly points us to the Lord of the church and to the heavenly nature of God's earthly people. The *structure* of the church is therefore God-centered. The church is not just another voluntary organization set up to accomplish whatever ends its organizers think most appropriate. The church is the community of God's saving rule, and the goals and forms of its ministry are determined by God.

The Goals of Ministry

What is the Lord's purpose in calling his people? Scripture presents a threefold purpose. The first is directed to the Lord himself—the church is called to be a worshiping assembly. We are a royal priesthood, a holy nation, a people for God's own possession that we may show forth the excellencies of him who called us out of darkness into his marvelous light (1 Pet. 2:9). Paul's apostolic calling had as its purpose the hymn of praise that would rise to God's name from the Gentiles (Rom. 15:8–6). Since the church is assembled before the Lord to praise him, the doxological

141

ministry of the church can never be a means to anything but the glory of God.

A second purpose of the ministry of the church is its service to the saints. We minister to God directly in worship; we minister to one another in Christian nurture. In Ephesians 4:12–26 Paul describes the ministry of nurture in the church. We grow together as we receive the ministry of the Word from those called of Christ to teach it. Those who minister to us enable us to minister to others. Development into maturity as Paul describes it is not an individual achievement: it involves the whole community of the church. It does not happen overnight, for growth involves struggle. We advance through testing as we understand and practice the truth together.

A third purpose of the ministry of the church is mission to the world. The church is called to witness. It is both a city set on a hill, to which the nations are drawn, and an army of ambassadors carrying the good news to the ends of the earth (Luke 24:28; Acts 5:32; Phil. 2:14–18; Matt. 28:18–20).

The calling of the church to minister directly to God, to the saints and to the world is one calling. Paul witnesses to the world of the Gentiles so that they may sing praise to God. Nurture and worship go together too: we sing to God in psalms, hymns and spiritual songs, but as we do so we teach and admonish one another (Col. 4:16; Eph. 5:19). When our hearts are filled with praise to God our very worship becomes a testimony to the world. At Pentecost the disciples praised God in many languages and their praise was a witness to those who heard. Evangelism is doxological.

The Means of Ministry

How are we to accomplish the goals of our ministry? Three means of ministry are presented in the New Testament. The first is the ministry of the Word. We are called to minister the truth of the gospel in faith and to faith (John 17:8, 17; Acts 6:4; Rom. 10:8; 1 Cor. 1:21; 2 Tim. 4:2; Titus 1:9). The growth of the church can be described as the growth of the word (Acts 12:24; 19:20). We are brought to birth by the Word of God preached to us (1 Pet. 1:23, 25) and nurtured by its ministry (Eph. 4:11, 12).

The second means is the ministry of order. This is closely associated with the faithful administration of the sacraments and includes the whole discipline of love in the body of Christ. The Word that is heard and believed must be obeyed. Mutual ministry within the church takes place in the caring of love. Paul condemns busybodies who traffic in other people's problems for their own satisfaction (1 Tim. 5:13) but he urges us to bear one another's burdens. In no other way can we fulfill Christ's command to love one another (Gal. 6:2). The discipline of the Spirit in the church is by no means limited to official acts of discipline. It is grounded in the faithfulness with which Christians encourage and counsel one another (Rom. 15:14). In baptism and the Lord's Supper the communion of the saints is displayed before the world as a witness. In these sacraments the church also submits to the Word of Christ in the ordering of his fellowship.

The ministry of mercy is the third way in which the ministry of the church is carried on. The teaching of the Word builds *faith*. The maintaining of order shows *love*. The ministry of mercy is a sign of *hope*. The miracles of Christ were signs of the Kingdom. They revealed the compassion of Christ and his purpose to deliver us from the curse, the penalty of sin. Jesus charged his disciples to feed the hungry, shelter the homeless, visit those who were sick or in prison. By ministering to their brothers and sisters in the Lord they would minister to the Lord himself (Matt. 25:31–46).

The parable of the Good Samaritan teaches us that the love that inspires sharing with the needy is modeled on the compassionate love of our Lord. It is the love of grace. We dare not ask, "Who is my neighbor?" in an effort to limit the number of those whom we are obliged to love. Rather we must ask, "To whom am I a neighbor? Where does God give me an opportunity to reveal love like the undeserved love by which I was saved?" The gospel of grace requires us to show compassion in Christ's name, first to the household of faith; then, as we have opportunity, to all men (Luke 10:3; Gal. 6:10).

Each of these three *means* of ministry serves each of the three *goals* of ministry. A computer of the right sort could quickly diagram this by constructing a small checkerboard square in which the three means laid off along one side would intersect the three purposes laid off along another side at right angles to the first. That is to say, the ministry of God's Word enables us to worship God with scriptural praise, to edify the saints and to witness to the world. So also does love order our worship of God, our life together and even our witness to the world, since we are a city set on a hill.

Finally, the ministry of mercy relates to the same three goals. It is part of our worship. Paul sees the offering to the poor in Jerusalem as an offering to God (2 Cor. 9:12–15; cf. Matt. 25:40). The ministry of mercy also serves the upbuilding of the saints. As the Judean poor received the ministry of their Gentile brethren, they learned to give thanks to God for his mercy to the Gentiles (2 Cor. 9:13, 14). The ministry of mercy also carries forward the witness of the gospel. Mission hospitals around the world have conveyed to many suspicious or hostile people the genuineness of Christian love.

The Forms of Ministry

With the purposes and means of the ministry of the church before us we may now ask, "Who are to conduct this ministry? How are they organized to do it?"

The answer is that those who minister in the church of Christ are called to their task by God. The author of Hebrews points out that no man could take the honor of the priesthood to himself but must be called by God as Aaron was (Heb. 5:4). As Christian brothers and sisters we have a heavenly calling, the calling of Jesus Christ, our great High Priest (Heb. 3:1).

Some Christians, reacting against the abuse of office in Christ's church, have held that all office was abolished with the passing of the Old Testament priesthood. In a sense almost the opposite is true. Far from there being no officers in the church of Christ, we are all officers in the church. Christ is our Mediator and great High Priest and we are united to him, sharing the blessing of his calling. The doctrine of the priesthood of all believers was precious to the Reformers and is no less important today.

On the other hand, while we have the blessings and benefits of Christ's priesthood, we cannot be priests as he is. The office of Christ is unique in the church. There is one Mediator between God and man, and one priest who has entered the sanctuary of heaven. Christ's authority is absolute. The power of the sword is his as the judge in heaven (Matt. 28:18; Acts 12:23). We do not now share Christ's rule over the world nor do we yet judge the world (1 Cor. 4:8; 6:2, 3). Yet we know that the ruler of the church is Lord of the world. In the church we experience the meaning of the new humanity that Christ came to redeem and establish. We therefore rejoice in his finished work as the second Adam.

Under the Lordship of Christ we are all called to minister to him, to one another and to the world. Every Christian is adopted in Christ, made a son or daughter of God by virtue of Christ's Sonship. At the same time, every Christian is called to a stewardship, a ministry. The Christian has both a *status* as a child of God and a *function* as a servant of the Kingdom.

His or her function is never carried out in isolation but always in the fellowship of Christ's body. This has been called the general office of all believers. The term may sound a little vague but its meaning is crucial. It means that every Christian is called of Christ and has a role to play in the work of the Kingdom. That role can be filled by no one else and carries with it the authority of Christ for its accomplishment.

Calling in the New Testament is always related to the gifts Christ has given us. Our spiritual gifts are not given for us to wrap in a napkin, but to use. The sphere that is defined by their use is the sphere of our calling. The apostle Paul used the expression: "I say by the grace given me…" (Rom. 12:3). What he means by that is, "I say as an apostle." It was the grace given to Paul that qualified him to be an apostle and to do the work of an apostle.

Every Christian has gifts for serving the Lord. Paul urges us to be sober and realistic in evaluating our gifts (Rom. 12:3). We must not be conceited, boasting of gifts that we do not possess, attempting to serve in spotlight roles for which we are unqualified. On the other hand, realism is not false modesty.

As we serve the Lord and know his blessing we become aware of gifts that we have received. It is not always easy (or necessary) to distinguish between natural and spiritual gifts. Our natural gifts have their source in the Creator Spirit and are renewed by the Spirit as we are made new creatures in Christ.

Prayerful reflection and discussion with friends will help us to identify our gifts. Yet we must realize that it is in service that our gifts will come to light. They are proved as we are approved and found pleasing to the Lord. Christ's servants are task-oriented: we hear the Great Commission and we set about the work of witness. We read the "one another" commands in the Epistles and we start to minister to other members of the body of Christ. We lead family prayer and are drawn into the joy of worship. We must be alert to the opportunities the Lord offers us and redeem the time. We are called to serve the Lord with zeal and imagination, looking and praying for open doors of service (2 Cor. 6:2; Eph. 5:15; Col. 1:9, 10; Phil. 1:10; Luke 12:35ff.).

Our individual gifts cause us to differ from others. For that very reason we should use them to serve others and receive the ministry of others. Only when the eye serves as an eye and the foot as a foot does the whole body enjoy the harmony of a created organism. Our own gifts form a pattern—in serving Christ our identity and our work come together. Like Peter we begin to fill out the name by which the Lord has called us.

As the Lord taught us in the parable of the Talents (Matt. 25:14–30) not all his servants have an equal number of gifts. What he requires is the faithful stewardship of what we have received. Those who have received gifts in greater degree bear greater responsibility.

In considering the means of ministry we saw that the Lord grants gifts for the ministry of the Word, of order and of mercy. Every Christian possesses some gifts in these areas. Every Christian must confess Christ's name before men (ministry of the Word in witness). Every Christian must encourage and admonish his fellow saints from the Bible (ministry of the Word in nurture). Every Christian must praise God in terms of scriptural revelation (ministry of the Word in worship). But some Christians are given unusual gifts for understanding God's Word and proclaiming it with authority. When a man has such gifts he will be fruitful in evangelism, in edifying the church and in lifting up the name of God in worship.

We may therefore distinguish between the general office of every believer and the special office of a man endued with the Spirit for the ministry of the gospel. When Paul speaks of the gifts of the Spirit he speaks also of the callings or offices that the exercise of such gifts involves (Rom. 12:3–8; 1 Cor. 12:28–30; Eph. 4:11). Some gifts of the Spirit require public recognition for their proper exercise. If a man gifted to preach the Word with authority is to be effective in that ministry in the midst of the church, the church must recognize the authority that God's calling gives him (Heb. 13:7, 17; Acts 20:28; 2 Tim. 4:2).

There are others besides ministers of the Word who have gifts for rule in the church and who must also be recognized as "elders"—older men who govern the Christian community (Titus 1:5; 1 Tim. 5:17). Since those who preach and teach with authority must also have gifts for rule, we speak of both teaching elders and ruling elders.

The ruling gift is distinguishable from the gift of teaching (Rom. 12:8; 1 Cor. 12:28). A man may have that gift and exercise it without being a teacher. In the Old Testament there were elders (representatives of the people) who were not priests or scribes (cf. Mark 14:43; Luke 7:3; 22:66). Paul distinguished between older men who rule well (ruling elders) and those who also labor in the Word and teaching (teaching elders). Elders of both kinds join in the rule of the church.

The ministry of mercy is carried out by those who have the gifts to be deacons. They must be able to show mercy with cheerfulness (Rom. 12:8). Paul gives additional qualifications for deacons in 1 Timothy 3:8–13.

Are the women mentioned in verse 11 also deacons? The requirements are virtually identical to the requirements in verse 8 and Paul does say, "in like manner." On the other hand, if many or most deacons were women why does Paul again say "deacons" in verse 12? Were the women deacons limited to widows over 60 who met the requirements given for enrollment in 1 Timothy 5:3–10? Paul calls Phoebe a deacon of the church that is at Cenchreae (Rom. 16:1). Even if the word is to be translated "servant" (it is masculine) it would seem that Phoebe is engaged in a ministry that requires the public recognition and support of the Roman church.

Paul clearly excludes women from the teaching office in connection with the principle that in the church family, as in the home, the woman is not to exercise authority over the man (1 Tim. 2:12; 1 Cor. 14:34, 35). If the diaconal office is seen as a serving office administering help and comfort for the poor and needy, it would contrast with the rule exercised by elders. The authority given to women in the office so conceived would be like that which Paul sought for Phoebe.

As we have seen, the office of apostle and of prophet laid the foundation for the church. These are offices that did not continue once the revelation of Jesus Christ to his church was complete. The other offices do continue with a great variety of giftedness within each one. Evangelists, pastors, teachers are all ministers of the Word according to their gifts. Deacons too may be gifted to administer the funds for the poor or more gifted in showing cheerfulness in the hospital ministry. The offices of teaching elder, ruling elder and deacon correspond to the ministry of the Word, of order and of mercy at the level of special office.

The mediatorial office of Jesus Christ is supreme in the church. From him the gifts for all the other offices are given. We may now add a vertical dimension to the checkerboard diagram of ministry, a dimension that will show the distinction between the general office of all believers at the base of the pyramid, the special office of ministers, elders and deacons in the middle, and the mediatorial office of Christ at the apex.

Of course, the diagram only indicates the *structure* of ministry in the church. It does not show the fire of the Spirit that gives life to the whole. The diagram helps us to see the richness of ministry in the church. It also shows that the special officers do not have gifts that differ in *kind* from the gifts of the general office but only in *degree*. By the mutual ministry of all these gifts of the Spirit the church of Christ functions as one body in his service.

AUTHORITY IN MINISTRY

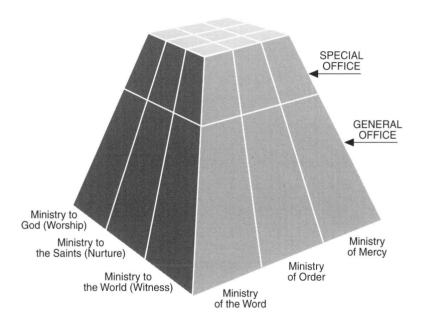

GOALS OF MINISTRY   MEANS OF MINISTRY

STRUCTURE OF MINISTRY OF THE CHURCH

NOTES

Chapter 1. The Goal of the Gospel

1. Hendriksen, William, *Exposition of the Pastoral Epistles* (Baker Book house, 1970), pp. 39, 40.

2. Quoted by William Childs Robinson in *The Word of the Cross* (The Sovereign Grace Union), p. 65.

3. Quoted by E. M. Blaiklock in *Layman's Answer* (Hodder and Stoughton, l968), p. 67.

4. Calvin, John, *Institutes of the Christian Religion*, Book II, Chapter VII, Paragraph 12 (italics added).

Chapter 2. Entrusted with the Good News

1. Iain Murray, *The Forgotten Spurgeon* (The Banner of Truth Trust, 1966), p. 44.

2. J. H. Merle d'Aubigné, *The Reformation in England*, vol. 1 (The Banner of Truth Trust, l971), p. 155.

3. Iain Murray, *The Forgotten Spurgeon* (The Banner of Truth Trust, 1966), p. 67.

Chapter 3. Shhh! They're Praying

1. *The Free Offer of the Gospel* (Presbyterian and Reformed, 1979), pp. 26, 27.

2. Quoted by William Fitch in *Enter into Life* (Eerdmans, 1961), pp. 35, 36.

3. David L. Edwards, *Evangelical Essentials: A Liberal-Evangelical Dialogue* (InterVarsity, 1988), pp. 128, 129.

Chapter 4. What's a Woman to Do?
1. George W. Knight III, *The New Testament Teaching on the Role Relationship of Men and Women* (Baker, 1977); James B. Hurley, *Man and Woman in Biblical Perspective* (Zondervan, 1981); John Piper and Wayne Grudem, editors, *Recovering Biblical Manhood and Womanhood* (Crossway Books, Wheaton, IL, 1991).

2. C. S. Lewis, *Mere Christianity* (The MacMillan Co, 1958), p. 84.

3. John Piper and Wayne Grudem, editors, *Recovering Biblical Manhood and Womanhood* (Crossway Books, Wheaton, IL, 1991), p. 70.

4. James B. Hurley, *Man and Woman in Biblical Perspective* (Zondervan, 1981), p. 216.

5. John Piper and Wayne Grudem, editors, *Recovering Biblical Manhood and Womanhood* (Crossway Books, Wheaton, IL, 1991), p. 192.

6. John Piper and Wayne Grudem, editors, *Recovering Biblical Manhood and Womanhood* (Crossway Books, Wheaton, IL, 1991), p. 56.

Chapter 5. Who's Qualified to Lead?
1. Hendriksen, William, *Exposition of the Pastoral Epistles* (Baker Book house, 1970), p. 129.

Chapter 6. Teachers, True and False
1. 1991 minutes of the 203rd General Assembly of the Presbyte-

rian Church (U.S.A.), Part 1, Journal, Pastoral Letter, p. 57,263.

2. Robert Short, *The Parables of Peanuts* (Harper and Row, 1968), p. 161.

3. O. Hallesby, *Conscience* (London: InterVarsity, 1962), pp. 98, 99.

Chapter 7. When You're a Young Leader

1. Randy C. Alcorn in "Strategies to Keep from Falling" from *Sins of the Body:* Ministry in a Sexual Society, Terry C. Muck, editor (Christianity Today and Word, 1989), pp. 118, 119.

Chapter 8. The Care and Nurture of Widows

1. John Murray, *Divorce* (Presbyterian and Reformed Publishing Company, 1980); Jay Adams, *Marriage, Divorce and Remarriage in the Bible* (Zondervan, 1995).

Chapter 9. How to Treat Your Elders

1. Larry Parker, *We Let Our Son Die* (Harvest House, 1980).

Chapter 10. Does It Pay to Serve God?

1. Kenneth Copeland, *The Laws of Prosperity* (Kenneth Copeland Publisher, 1974), p. 67.

2. D. R. McConnell, *A Different Gospel* (Massachusetts: Hendrickson Publisher, 1988), p. 180.

3. Charles Hodge, *A Commentary on the Second Epistle to the Corinthians, An Exposition* (Banner of Truth Trust, 1959), p. 219.

4. Jeremiah Burroughs, *The Rare Jewel of Christian Contentment* (Banner of Truth Trust, 1964), p. 19.

5. "Things Don't Just Happen," a poem by Mrs. Charles Lee.

6. James Paton, *The Story of John G. Paton Told for Young Folks* (A. L. Burt Co., 1892), p. 74.

7. "Betrayal" by Hester H. Cholmondeley, a 19th century poet.

Chapter 11. A Charge to a Man of God
1. J. C. Ryle, *Never Perish* (Grand Rapids: Evangelical Press, n.d.), p. 7.

2. Henry Van Dyke, *The Lost Word* (Scribner's, 1939).

3. "Fight the Good Fight" by John S. B. Monsell.

Chapter 12. Using Riches Properly
1. Ronald S. Wallace, *Calvin's Doctrine of the Christian Life*, pp. 170– 177.

2. William Law, *A Serious Call to a Devout and Holy Life* (Sovereign Grace Publishers, 1971), pp. 28 ff.

Appendix
1. This appendix is reprinted by permission of Edmund P. Clowney, author of *Living in Christ's Church* (Great Commission Publications, 1986), in which it appears as chapter 12.

BIBLIOGRAPHY

Blaiklock, E. M. *Layman's Answer.* London: Hodder and Stoughton, 1968.

Burroughs, Jeremiah. *The Rare Jewel of Christian Contentment.* London: Banner of Truth Trust, 1964.

Calvin, John. *Institutes of the Christian Religion.* Vol. 1. John T. McNeill, editor, Philadelphia: The Westminster Press, 1960.

Clowney, Edmund P. *Living in Christ's Church.* Great Commission Publications, 1986.

D'Aubigné, J. H. Merle. *The Reformation in England.* Vol. 1. London: The Banner of Truth Trust, 1971

Edwards, David L. and Stott, John. *Essentials—A Liberal-Evangelical Dialogue.* London: Hodder and Stoughton, 1988.

Hallesby, 0. *Conscience.* London: InterVarsity Press, 1962.

Hendriksen, William. *Exposition of the Pastoral Epistles.* New Testament Commentary. Grand Rapids: Baker Book House, 1970.

Hodge, Charles. A *Commentary on the Second Epistle to the Corinthians.* London: Banner of Truth Trust, 1959.

Law, William. A *Serious Call to a Devout and Holy Life.* Grand Rapids: Sovereign Grace Publishers, 1971.

McConnell, D. R. *A Different Gospel.* Massachusetts: Hendrickson Publishers, 1988.

Muck, Terry C., editor. *Sins of the Body:* Ministry in a Sexual Society. Christianity Today and Word, 1989.

Murray, Iain H. *The Forgotten Spurgeon.* London: The Banner of Truth Trust, 1966.

Murray, John and Ned B. Stonehouse. *The Free Offer of the Gospel.* New Jersey: Presbyterian and Reformed Publishing Company, 1980.

Paton, James. *The Story of John G. Paton Told For Young Folks.* A. L. Burt Company, 1892.

Robinson, John A. T. *But That I Can't Believe!* New York: The New American Library, 1967.

Ryle, J. C. *Never Perish.* Grand Rapids: Evangelical Press, n.d.